This is a version of the story. I was born January 6, 1965 as Eric Martin Enquist. My mother and father, Patricia May Gorman (Enquist) and Lynn Martin Enquist, were young, and divorced a year later. He died in a car accident in the summer of 1968, which coincided with my adoption and name change to John Jerome Gallaher, Jr. The first complication in this story is that my adoptive mother, Kathleen Patricia Sullivan (Gallaher), when I was born, was my second cousin. Her father, Timothy Tade Sullivan, and my birth grandmother, Hazel Belle Sullivan (Enquist), were siblings. The second twist is that my brother, Richard, who I was raised with, also adopted, was, at birth, my cousin. His birth mother and my birth father were siblings. It should have been an easy story to sort out, but it took fifty years.

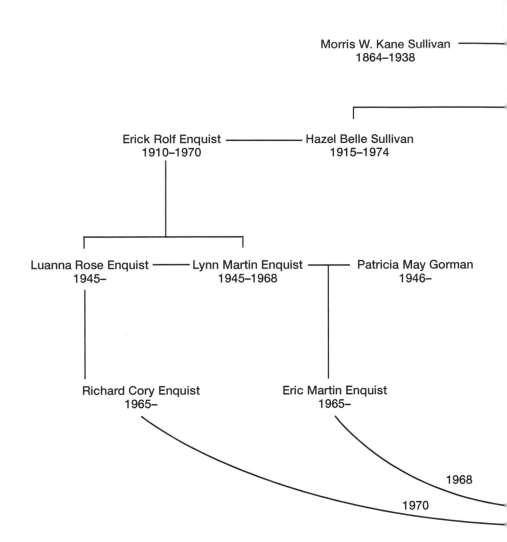

Morris W. Kane Sullivan
1864–1938

Erick Rolf Enquist ——————— Hazel Belle Sullivan
1910–1970   1915–1974

Luanna Rose Enquist ——— Lynn Martin Enquist ——— Patricia May Gorman
1945–   1945–1968   1946–

Richard Cory Enquist   Eric Martin Enquist
1965–   1965–

1968

1970

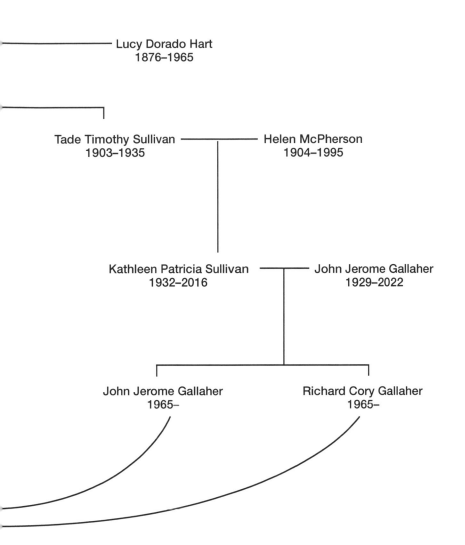

Lucy Dorado Hart
1876–1965

Tade Timothy Sullivan ——————— Helen McPherson
1903–1935   1904–1995

Kathleen Patricia Sullivan ——— John Jerome Gallaher
1932–2016   1929–2022

John Jerome Gallaher   Richard Cory Gallaher
1965–   1965–

MY LIFE
IN BRUTALIST
ARCHITECTURE

ALSO BY JOHN GALLAHER

Gentlemen in Turbans, Ladies in Cauls

The Little Book of Guesses

Map of the Folded World

Your Father on the Train of Ghosts, with G.C. Waldrep

In a Landscape

Ghost/Landscape, with Kristina Marie Darling

Brand New Spacesuit

The Monkey and the Wrench: Essays Into Contemporary Poetry, with Mary Biddinger

Time Is a Toy: The Selected Poems of Michael Benedikt, with Laura Boss

MY LIFE IN BRUTALIST ARCHITECTURE

POEMS

JOHN GALLAHER

FOUR WAY BOOKS
TRIBECA

LIBRARY OF CONGRESS CATALOGING-IN-PUBLICATION DATA

Names: Gallaher, John, 1965- author.

Title: My life in brutalist architecture : poems / John Gallaher.

Description: New York : Four Way Books, 2024.

Identifiers: LCCN 2023031688 (print) | LCCN 2023031689 (ebook) | ISBN 9781954245846 (trade paperback) | ISBN 9781954245853 (ebook)

Subjects: LCGFT: Poetry.

Classification: LCC PS3607.A415 M9 2024 (print) | LCC PS3607.A415 (ebook) | DDC 811/.6--dc23/eng/20230724

LC record available at https://lccn.loc.gov/2023031688

LC ebook record available at https://lccn.loc.gov/2023031689

This book is manufactured in the United States of America and printed on acid-free paper.

Four Way Books is a not-for-profit literary press. We are grateful for the assistance we receive from individual donors, public arts agencies, and private foundations including the NEA, NEA Cares, Literary Arts Emergency Fund, and the New York State Council on the Arts, a state agency.

[clmp]

We are a proud member of the Community of Literary Magazines and Presses.

This book is dedicated to the adoptees.

There is something temptingly tidy about the idea of adoption: a family with extra love and resources meets a child in desperate need of both. The happy ending almost writes itself.

—RUTH GRAHAM, *The Atlantic*

"What is your story?"
"Ours, insofar as it is absent."

—EDMOND JABÈS, trans. Rosmarie Waldrop

ARCHITECTURES

*

*

*

Family medical history: ☐ Unknown / Adopted

One clue might be attachment theory, which holds that a strong bond with at least one nurturing adult—usually the mother—is essential to a child thriving . . . Infants and toddlers with a so-called "disorganized attachment". . . are more psychologically vulnerable later in life.

—Olga Khazan, *The Atlantic*

Survey questions. Was this child in an unsafe situation? Should they have a new name that is unknown to their biological family?

When my daughter was born, I took the only picture I had from before my adoption out of its frame to take a picture of it, and on the back, in spidery, unfamiliar handwriting was "Marty, nine mos." I appear next as John, three-and-a-half, and Marty disappears, a ghost name.

I found my birth name later, going through medical and legal forms when my father had a heart attack in 2013. It was the original, yellowed, adoption record. . . . How many years of not thinking "Oh, you know, we could check that." The details of March 18, 1968. In the matter of Eric Martin Enquist, a minor.

And so, then, what does the self consist of?

The theme is time. The theme is unspooling.

* blood of my blood

Ghostwalk, Missouri

Our neighbor to the left had a stroke a couple years ago. It didn't look
like he was going to make it, and then he made it. I'm watching him
from my window as he makes his slow way across his yard
with some tree branches that fell in last night's storm. Three steps.
Wait. Three steps. It's a hard slog. Watching, I want to pitch in.
And we do, at such times, wanting to help. But on the other hand,
it's good to be as physical as possible in recovery. Maybe this is part
of his rehab. Maybe this is doctor's orders: DO YARDWORK.
And here comes his wife across the yard anyway, to give a hand
with a large branch. She's able to quickly overtake him, and she folds
into the process smoothly, no words between them that I can make out.
It's another part of what makes us human, weighing the theory of mind,
watching each other struggle or perform, anticipating each other's
thoughts, as the abject hovers uncannily in the background, threatening
to break through the fragile borders of the self. "What's it like to be
a bat?" we ask. The bats don't respond. How one life unfolds
at the periphery of catastrophes happening to others. I'm
reading, while my neighbor struggles, that the squirrel population
in New England is in the midst of an unprecedented boom. A recent
abundance of acorns is the reason for this surge in squirrel populations,
most particularly in New Hampshire. They're everywhere, being
squirrely, squirreling acorns away. We call it "Squirrelnado" because
it's all around us, circling, and dangerous, and kind of funny. Language
springs from the land, and through our imagination, we become
human. They're back in the house now. We name the things we see,
or they name themselves into our experience, whichever, and then
we use those names for things we don't understand, what we can't
express. Wind becomes spirit becomes ghost. Mountain becomes
god. The land springs up before us. It shakes us and pushes us over.

Coded Messages

The purpose of life is to carry a sequence of code. And so,
being adopted, I'm part of a plot, a sleeper cell
in enemy territory, quietly working against the system
from within. My password is "My Life in Brutalist Architecture."
It's fall, I'm on an ancestry website, signing up for a DNA kit.
"Let's give science a try!" I'm a commercial, I'm a how-to video,
I'm a Getty Image of a clean kitchen and a Prezi slideshow
clicking through several collection kits to choose from,
flow chart questions leading from cousins to health risks. Bits and pieces of a story,
better than no story, like saying we drove through Grant City once,
and that's what becomes of Grant City, light of the body, light
of the dreaming of the body. I've dwelt in the kingdom
of absence, living in two directions, or no directions,

like hunting the snark, when there is no snark,
as all snarks are boojums. It's endless. Then gone. Some many-eyed angel
of possibility. There are a lot of John Gallahers out there.
I'm friends with several on social media, and I get updates:
John Gallaher flying, John Gallaher at the pyramids, etcetera.
And there are several Eric Enquists, the birth name
I found in a drawer. It was scrambled, like the idea
that there is one right and true name, like the idea
that if you never speak a name, it never existed.
I didn't friend any Eric Enquists on social media. That
didn't seem funny, in the way that sending a friend request to John Gallaher
felt funny: "Hey, John, it's John! What are we up to?"
Whatever you call yourself, though, it's the same sequence of code.
Dear rose, dear octopus, it's a dramatization: you belong

where you are and you belong to something else. Fire. Element. This is why I'm doing it. It's like how it turns out humans might be the most remarkable thing in the universe, and the price for that would be that we're the only ones who would know.

Everything I Know about Portland, OR

I wandered invisibly, the blank idea of the body double, until,
at three, I stepped alone
from a Continental jet with a golden tail,
in a gray plaid jacket and matching hat, pressed
into an idea, the way Portland is an idea, time and place, the one thing
they didn't change on the birth certificate. The one thing
I could know, Portland, my diamond. Welcome
to the process, how we're all part of some two-point process, transformed
through the screen of the other's imagination, reduced
to a means, which vivifies one's exterior and makes of it
the plastic and pictorial world. I was born on the Feast of the Epiphany,
so I have these sudden and striking realizations,
which is a terrible way to say "in the course
of human events," but you use what you have, as the Feast
of the Epiphany asks, "What more is there to a person

than what is seen?"

What is seen—Rock and plant alive with it. Organs exchanging organs
alive with it. The path through Portland, and the counter-path
through Portland, as someone falls asleep while driving
and crashes on Bluff Rd. Bluff Rd., like it's a joke, a slow-motion arc
into the trees of 1968. This is how my father dies, out looking for my mother,
whose name no one remembers (as told to me

by my adoptive parents
over fried clams, Howard Johnsons, 1976).

That's all I know of Portland, which got its name when Asa Lovejoy
and Francis Pettygrove flipped a coin in 1845. Now I'm wearing
my John Gallaher mask. The adopted child couldn't master hardness,

so it opted for distance. "Look," the map says, "you could have remembered them

        if you were paying better attention."

What, don't you think I've been saying this all my life?

1968 as Superhero Origin Story, *Et Alia*

Look, up in the sky! Look what the culture is thinking of itself!
Two orphans up against it, ladies and gentlemen. And aren't we all orphans
in some way? Don't we want to be? The alien falls to earth
in a ball of fire. The wealthy child watches again and again
as his parents are murdered. We'll stop there, as the rest
is all newspapers and money, the ability to fly
and the metaphor of falling. Night arrives. Exterior. I'm three years old
and I'm not allowed to fly alone, so the family makes arrangements with a man
to sit next to me, because it's important to have someone
to sit next to. Your Alfred. Your Ma and Pa Kent. Aunt May.
The pilot gives me some pin-on golden wings,
because in 1968, cockpits are open, inviting places,
as if you can just sit down and say, "Let's go," and it's off
to Kansas, clicking one's heels, imagining home,
though I had no say in the matter.

*

The adopted child dreams of Superman, but the dream
is Batman just as much, or Spiderman. I don't
remember his backstory. Something traumatic, I suppose.
Because you have to be working to avenge the past,
to redeem yourself, or to prove yourself
worthy. A lot of people are lost this way, though I could
just as easily have said, "found." I forget
the exact economy of superheroes, having given them up
for cowboys, who just want

                       some obscure horizon

to squint at.

American Travelogue

After the plane lands, late in the baby scoop era, 1945–72
as I'm being driven to My New Life, I call out, frantic
for my PEZ candy dispensers, pronouncing it "peas,"
and my New Parents think I have to pee. They told this story
for years, about how funny I was. Hey, everybody,
Britney Spears says there are two kinds of people:
those who bring the show, and the audience. I'm disconsolate
about my PEZ,
and they're trying to teach me my new name.
It's "Hey, You"
                    or "TBD."
Absence is the necessary part.
                                        Out the window,
there's fog over the pond, and it feels like the spirit
rising. As we become builders by building, painters
by painting; so, too, we become spirit
by doing spirit acts, by water, by dust, brave
by weight and walls, and 12 candy pieces. I hear voices.
I have only to walk by a thrift shop, antique shop, and the PEZ Sailor
and PEZ Boy with Cap pipe up: *Aye, these briny waves!*
Golly, Sam, what's gotten into us? On YouTube,
there's a video of a rainstorm over a valley, sped up
so the rain comes down like it's pouring out of a bucket.
It splashes along the ridge. Sped up again, houses are sucked into the earth.
And again, and the mountains are waves, cresting and breaking,
Lil Bad Wolf chuckling in the background.

Driving home tonight I see the hardware store is having a sale
on buckets. If you'd like a deal on buckets,

call me: 853-8655. I can point to the sky, and tell you
where I came from.
                    I was brought by aliens, and I'd report back
by saying, "Report to ship now," which would upload,
since the last report, these fragments, the consolation
of objects in a row along the windowsill. Casper.
Sheriff Yellow. Goofy. It became a kind of joke, but I kept it up
for years, as one who no longer believes,
who goes to church anyway, repeats the incantation, sings.

Instructions for Performance

In the comedy version, I go with "I'm my own second cousin," adopted
by the daughter of the brother of my paternal grandmother. It's a kind of music:
      daughter of the brother of my paternal grandmother.
In the sad version, I'm three, my father's dead, and soon after, his
father and mother, with my birth mother lost
in my new parents' fear that she might hire a lawyer. Pitiful fear
that swallows states and pictures. I'm a recast character, dropped in,
season three, gray city in Brutalist architecture. The theme
                          is silence.

This is my class report. I stayed up all night working on the tri-fold.
"The theme is gratitude," The Adoption Story says. Monday
gratitude. Tuesday gratitude. Am I performing gratitude sufficiently?
Dial 1-800-ADOPTEE.

Pessoa, José tells me at The Pub last week, writes, "I have an altar
for every god
                in every corner of my soul." I get it, spitting
into a tube, watching the DNA online process arrow
story through Received, Extracted, Analyzing.
Like waiting for pizza delivery, only I'm the pizza. Death

phones, whispers, "Double cheese."

Because what are we anyway? Waiting.
Like "three ghosts" or "thought's prayer." And what do I say?
That I got cold once when I was a child, and never got warm?

Your Sport

"You should write a book about it," Margo says when she hears
I'm my own second cousin, though, in general, the story's not rare,
and Margo herself has a theory, maybe she's really her own cousin, as well.
Her mother's tall, dark hair, angular, and Margo's short,
blonde, and looks like her mother's younger sister
who would've been a teenager when she was born. "Someday,"
she says, "they'll fess up." I wonder if she means it,
or if this is the joke, where "Ha!" we say, one sibling to another,
"you're really adopted, and your *real* father is [insert name
of creepy neighbor]." Imprecisely, 2%
of the U.S. population is adopted, the National Conference
of State Legislatures tells us, sailing across a sea of hot takes
and glamorous advertising. There's this T-shirt I like,
that I see around on runners, it goes:
YOUR SPORT'S PUNISHMENT IS MY SPORT.
Here's an adoptee T-shirt idea: my condition in this world
is your punishment, terrifying revelation, punchline.
(Maybe there could be check boxes:

                              "Choose one")

*

There's an advertisement at the gym to adopt a rescue dog. "Woof,"
Time says. My brother is anyone. My sister
is anyone. My mother is every woman I pass
on the way to a coffee shop. It's a ready-made.
It's postmodern theory. I'll name it "The Charnel House,"
because that sounds like it could be the name of a coffee shop,
"Charnel House Coffee," but it's funny, right, because a charnel house
is really a vault of leftover bones. Bastard bones. We sort them

into boxes and call it unity. The adopted child
is a category. It's like cutting pictures from magazines: box
of houses, box of people running, box of sky.

Conversation with My Fear

Last night I was eating glass again. I'm still thinking about it,
contemplating this turkey sandwich. "Well, hero,
whatcha gonna do?" I ask, and eat.
That bad dreams happen to everyone is no consolation.
That my mind is racing is no consolation. I built my fear
a house in Brutalist architecture, its utilitarian designs
dictated by function over form, raw materials
and the mundane left exposed. And I kneel
at the feet of my fear. My fear says
these people don't love me, they adopted me by mistake,
little brown-headed cowbird, and whispers at night
in paperwork scattered around the house.
"On one of these pages, your true name is inscribed,
adrift in a sea of blood and ink," it says. I was three,
just getting used to things. But change remains,
so now I want to change my name weekly. Episodic.
As all names are made-up names. I want to be weather.
I want a name that rhymes with "orange."
I used to think I was a robot boy, a name of buzzing wires,
my headaches as gears skipping broken teeth.
It's been a rough few years. Everyone I know is barely
holding it together. Don't worry, we say. Or don't worry
so much. When what we really mean is, actually, now
that I think about it, yes, worry. Worry constantly. Panic. Never stop.
And don't forget to sign up for the small sounds
you hear in the house, 2 a.m., as life is a lonely fight.
Like fighting my dead father and mother in their locked boxes,
travelling all the directions at once. Their photos in the album
always win. Obvious as a birthday cake, the things I've done

to charm myself, there on the porch chatting away
with my fear. "No, this isn't the way to do it at all,"
my fear says, "Do I have to show you everything?"

The Provenance of Salt

"Is this a weed or a flower?" Time asks the adopted child.
As the account one produces of the world is different from another's,
is there no way of knowing what is the case?

                             For instance,
at my mother's funeral, the director walks my brother and me
through the steps of the service checklist: 1) Song 2) Candle.
She asks if we've done this before, or if this is our first time,
and I say, no, this is the only time
our mother has died. I feel kind of bad about it now, the look
on her face, but my brother laughed. And, both adopted, we'd no idea
if this was the first or not, so, hard joke, friend.
 "So, how did we get to this point again?" Time asks. And then
we practice our fragility, plotting the non-people,
non-disasters. "Difficulty Forming Emotional Attachments"
is step three on the Impact of Adoption list. Have you
thought about this as a Markov process,

                             with a set of states and transitions?
My brother wants to know why I care,
the DNA, birth, what my name was. What is fundamental—

We see the world, but the world is in the looking,
a goodbye to the definition one has of oneself and hello
to a burning field.

                  Time asks if its transitory nature undermines
its worth, or might that very brevity be part of its importance. Perhaps
I've stepped on too many cracks. More people,
more information. Perhaps this is the correct response
to the bureaucracy of services, as it's better to have a process you love
than to have a goal you want to achieve. If you love the process,

you're always in that toward which you are aiming. If it's the goal you're aiming for, it's always going to be ahead or behind.

It's the error in conceptions like "the ends justify the means." The means are where you dwell. The means are every person you love.

Division

Let's watch the process one more time. During the first stage
of mitosis, prophase, we see the classic chromosome structure.
Notice the DNA condensing. Outside, my neighbor
is watering the new tree they planted
to replace the one they had to remove, and in both her and the tree
microtubules are appearing and the nuclear membrane
is breaking down. The tightrope choreography:
metaphase, when the chromosomes are aligned
at the center of the cell, or anaphase, as the chromosomes
are moving apart. Telophase is then marked by the appearance
of new nuclear membranes. And this is the end
of mitosis. About 80 minutes, and two new cells
are ready to grow and perform their specialized functions.
It's complicated. Or maybe it isn't so complicated.

I wasn't there when my mother died. My brother Richard and I
had been there, called by our dad, when her organs
started shutting down. But when we got there, she rallied,
her organs started functioning again, and we had work,
so we left. And then she died, wax statue, Alzheimer's, stroke, coma.
The Earth is no home, Bierbichler says.
So, where is your home? And who is there?
And what is your relation to who is there? Your human relation.
My father sits in the empty house. It's become his meal of rocks.

My mother is the universe now, who once
told us that if she "went senile,"
we were to take her out to the backyard and shoot her.

She didn't mean it, but what someone means at a moment like this
is also complicated, as the slow milling of the oceans
and land, geese rising from a lake
and back down, some clock beneath these hills.

Nest I

A few months before my mother died, there was a storm
that blew the bird's nest we'd been watching out of the redbud
in our front yard. The eggs had just hatched. The nest was too low,
just over head height, and there wasn't a lot of protection. I was sure
a cat would get up there. Birds make mistakes with their nests
all the time. And here it was, on the lawn ten feet or so
from the front door, right side up. Two dead chicks
on either side. But, amazingly, one very alive chick still in the nest,
face up to the sky, imploring. And suddenly this is the most
important thing there is, that there's ever been.

                                                Problem two.
I have a towel, fresh from the laundry, smelling like spring breeze
laundry sheets, and it becomes a kind of sling I wrap
around two limbs, and I have to keep walking past the nest
on the ground while I work, the dead and living, side by side.
I've no idea if this is working, what the birds
will think of this, only that I imagine I've a narrow window
to work in, that somewhere around here,
the parent birds are watching, though they might have left,
or they might be dead. And then I'm holding this nest
a foot from my face, going up the ladder, this very small face
inches from mine, looking up, open.

                                                It's a world filled
with hunger. I don't know how else to say it. Then, nest
and bird placed in the tree, I'm stepping back around the dead.
That's it. The birds return. I don't mow that part of the lawn
for weeks. The bird grows and flies off. My mother dies.
I leave the towel in the tree thirteen months. Every time
I go to take it down, I do something else instead,
until one day that seems otherwise like any other day.

Your Innocence Will Not Protect You

There's no nostalgia like this shirt, whispering "1976" with blocky
red-white-blue, fife and drum, bicentennial print my mother
sewed for me and my brother. Two little adopted boys, unalike as moon
and wrench, born two days apart, transplanted into matching shirts.
The questions that follow "if you don't mind my asking," include the word "real"
and it's my job to make no one upset or uncomfortable.
To wear difference and to wear sameness. A life of "I don't mind."

I really want to know where those shirts went. To touch them. Because
letting go is beyond me. Because I'm next.
And then you. This house. The sun. Friends, it's almost yesterday.
Don't you feel it? So call your mother from a pay phone
or imagine calling your mother from a pay phone, even if
you have to imagine a mother. Best if you have to imagine a mother,
then you know you're really onto something. Better still if you have
to imagine a pay phone. Best if everything's imagined: silver disco spacesuits,
the working day of a herring fishing fleet as it sets sail
from the Shetland Islands, doctor's visits, and grand metaphors
from swinging French ye-ye. How quaint we were.
                                                    How many ways
we have to avoid ourselves. And where am I in all of this? Or better,
any of us, you, assembled or guessed or made up, in a chair, reading,
and you notice the time. In advertisements, it was always 10:10
because 10:10 looked elegant on a dial. I saw 10:10 on a digital clock
in an advertisement just now, which reminded me of this,
and I wondered if it's just convention,
or if someone thinks 10:10 is still elegant in digital. It's like being the best
person in town at Rubik's Cube. You could've had a shot at TV
if this were 1976. But now
look at you. You get to call it art.

Reliquariana

A reliquary has come to mean any container of relics, but we think of them
     most often
as a container of the bones of saints: the left arm bones
of the levitating philosopher-saint, Thomas Aquinas, are kept
in a thirteenth-century Neapolitan basilica, and so on. Occasionally,
they make the news, as when the stolen brain of the patron saint of magicians
was found in the thief's kettle. There's one close to me, outside Maryville,
in a monastery in the small town of Conception. I've never been,
as knowing "Conception contains a reliquary"
is enough. If one, as they say, dies as a library fire, one is born, then,
a reliquary. "I myself am a reliquary," we can say, as the devil
is in the details.

"Where did my family go?" the adopted child asks.
"I am your family," distance replies.

I dream I'm being chased through the woods,
which the dream bible tells us means there's some anxiety
in your life that you're fleeing, maybe by pretending there's no issue,
or it's the wrong issue or person, like how,
in 1997, a guy named Jason Rockman feels this need to send an envelope
with his business card (he was a CPA), along with school pictures of two girls,
about ten and fifteen, to my brother Richard in Virginia Beach.
Since we're adopted, all envelopes of unmarked pictures are at least a little
     mysterious,
so he held onto it for thirty years, though he never asked why it was sent,
who these people were. He showed it to me last year, thinking maybe
it was a clue. Because the adopted are used to living in a mystery novel.
"A clue to what?"

*

Reliquaries also have remainder bins, unmarked bits,
and when you just appear in this world, orphan or adoptee,
there's a hole you balance over on your apparatus of bones,
mystery bones that you chase or flee or excavate
and then carefully place back in the envelope and put away.

Your Number

Heroic meaning is in the other room eating bacon
as I'm returning from my health risk assessment screening.
I usually faint with needles. They say it's anxiety, and I apologize,
because it scares people when my blood pressure drops to 60 / 35
and my eyes roll. To distract me, the phlebotomist recounts
the stand-up comedy career she's hoping to get going,
centered around her life as a senior citizen. "Dementia
keeps people guessing," she says, so she has a lot to work with.
But there's courage in that, too, the way my mother
talked about Old Timer's Disease, the way she called Scenic Hills,
where she lived her last 30 years, "Senile Hills."
So we assess the risks. Statistical analysis.

This is the grand procession of the stars: you blink, and the nurse
calls your number. Stan Lee died today. So the meaning
of today is "Stan Lee." Comic books. Superheroes. It's game
time. The #1 song on the day you were born is the meaning
of your life. Wednesday, January 6th, 1965:
"I Feel Fine," by The Beatles,

                              is the meaning of my life.
My total cholesterol is 197, and my HDL is 78, a natural history
of sitting by this window, holding my screening summary
like the book of daily prayer. I'm not religious, so this is what I get,
along with the selected poems of John Ashbery. Thank you,
screening summary, it all makes sense now. My glucose is 93.
I was fasting, mostly, though I forgot and had a cup of coffee
and some grapes. The receptionist said that's fine.
Thank you, receptionist, who says that's fine, by The Beatles,
1965. My blood pressure is 108/56. My BMI is 23. Thank you,

O happy asemic summer days carrying us along
in a fog of flies. And then it's November, and it's just me
and this one fly, circling the health screening room, low
slow arcs, that I'm naming The Soul, or maybe Stan, as it tilts by.

In the Prayer of Quiet, One Erases All Things

As ontogeny recapitulates phylogeny, or *nomen est omen,* my mother
would wake me up singing "Good morning, good mooooorrning!"
and I hated it. Now she's gone, and I wake the kids
 singing "Good morning, good mooooorning!"
One fewer "r" in morning. It's how I'm an original. The answer
to the question "Is it nature or nurture?" is "Yes."

                                                            Today
I went for a drive. They've just put up a wind farm
in the cornfields north of town. I feel it's been there forever,
blinking red lights. I turn, and they've put up a windfarm
to the south of town. I'm related to this map, once removed.
I'm a mystic of the colors beige, gray, and taupe. "The dancer
is the distance between language and metaphor"
is what I should say, but I say, "I'm my own second cousin!
Let me tell you the story." I have several versions
to choose from. "Toxic Positivity Day"
is one. "What would you have done?" is another.
In my theory of the universe, all adoptees are a secret family.
We meet in dreams, and understand belonging,
each to each, in the lacquer garden.

It's my glass prayer. It's like that feeling of falling
I get on balconies. It's exactly
like that in everywayforeveramen,
vagabonding memory and image.

                                        Or is it just
the distance going on and on that looks that way?

Family Projects

It's Day of the Dead Week at the middle school and they're doing projects
on family members who've died. What they liked. Five words
that describe them. A picture. One of the kids wants to use their sister
who died at birth, only there are no pictures, no five words, things
they liked. The teacher starts crying. So now the class is doing pets.
Luke's son, Isaac, was crying last night, about Wesley, his grandparents' dog,
but Wesley's been dead over a year, and they only saw him
Christmas and summer. It's always about more than it's about,
as Eliot's at the kitchen counter, gluing a picture of our cat Chatty
to the info sheet. He's allergic to cats, we found out, and so after Chatty died,
we've gotten no more cats. The death of Chatty is the death of all cats,
the death of an idea. He asks if there's a way he might someday
no longer be allergic. He thinks about it a lot.

Thus ends my research for today. I want to go for a walk, maybe
take some pictures of the trees before the rusting colors of fall
are gone. We've one in our front yard, the one with the bird nest
that fell out, that I replaced. It has incredible bright red leaves
right now. But it's 34 degrees, so it's a quick photo and burst
back inside. Our house is almost a hundred years old, first
on the block. It was on Main Street, then carted here in the 40s
by a veterinarian or pediatrician, to what then was "out-of-town."
Now there are neighborhoods another mile. We're the fourth owners
of this house. When we moved in, we brought a nurse's hat
we found on a shelf in a closet in our last house, even older, which
we were told was haunted, and placed it on a shelf in our new closet.

Haunted Mansion ride. October night.

Town Crier

Life was rough for a lot of people in 1794. And, okay, everything is relative,
but when I shake a bottle of Zesty Italian dressing
to watch the jumble sorted into oil and vinegar again,
it only separates into two things,
and that's too simple for my fuzzy reflection
in the refrigerator's silver door,
a gray blur I can imagine is my body
rising from a lake in winter, 1794, with some drunk
and sardonic self-appointed town-crier stumbling in.
YOU BREATHED IN AND OUT A BUNCH OF TIMES
AND THEN DIED, he cries,
                              shaking his bell.
In the beginning, you're given a name, but spelling is moody,
so Peter Bucher is Peter Beougher, Booher, Booker, etc., from his birth
in Germany, 1725, to his death in Pennsylvania, circa 1794.
Look, I have some time to kill, waiting on my DNA results.
I'm sorry. The way my parents were sorry for not remembering
what my name was before I was adopted, and then telling me,
but getting it wrong, and joking, "I guess we'll keep you anyway."

We joke with those we love. Even a flea market find. I'm
sorry. Your neighbor's had a stroke. I'm sorry. There's been
an accident. I'm sorry. I returned, and saw under the sun, that the race
is not to the swift, nor the battle to the strong, neither yet bread
to the wise, nor yet riches to those of understanding, nor yet favour
to those of skill; but time and chance happeneth to all.
In paraphrase, Ecclesiastes 9:11. I'm sorry
                              I'm paraphrasing.
The past shifts with how we think of it. 1968. Life was hard
for a lot of people then, as well. Look
around. You're in the wilderness.

The Aura Homily

I was at a party where there was a person who could see auras,
who went around the room naming them. Silver Kathleen.
Etc. When it came to me, I didn't have one. How can one
not have an aura? Isn't it like not having a soul or something?
Is it because I'm adopted? Am I a chimera? Little blank aura kid?
I'm being a little defensive, I'm told. But why not just make
something up for me? Help a person out? Would it be that hard
to say, "Hmm, maybe it's a minty green"? Where's the harm?
These others look so happy with their auras. Well-adjusted,
bright-eyed. This website I'm on, because this is what's become of me,
lists ten possible auras and I've never felt more American,
an auraless adoptee reading "techniques from Buddhist monks
for your next two-week self-actualization workshop." Floating monks
reading by the glow of their auras. Let's talk parameters.

I took the Myers-Briggs test on my lunch break today,
and I'm an INTP, the laziest and most condescending
of the sixteen personality types, also the most likely type
to say black is my favorite color. Maybe I could call that
my aura. Adoptees are good at making stuff up.
Nuns, priests, and the void wear black. Maybe someone
would see me and think I'm a nun, priest, or the void. I mean,
I don't even believe in auras. And now, look at me.
Maybe, being adopted, my aura is lost in transit, UPS color,
wrong address color. Maybe my aura's a color that's not been invented yet,
a secret color, like how Homer couldn't see the color blue,
so the ocean was wine. Maybe it said, "Je est an autre" as it passed
and no one at this party speaks French, or the cortege
took a wrong turn, and said, sure, this place looks as good as any.

Time Is an Emotion

My adoptive parents told me my birth father died on the 4th of July.
It was my one fact. It grew tight as a house
I could curl up in. Later, when I was in high school,
I got a picture, gray and airless as the moon. Later,
I got upset and ripped it into four strips. Then I regretted it,
and taped it back together. And I know what this means. It means
I'm upset. It means dying is the great ephemeration. All that is us
goes on to live some other way, in pieces, for a teenager
to pin to a wall above their desk. The father frozen in amber.
Dear ornamental father. Me and my constituents
will be over here, talking things over, we say,
but to others it sounds more like

                              "Hi, my name is."

They almost got it, my parents. He died on July 9th.
That's pretty close. If I were writing a poem about America,
maybe I'd leave it. It's OK to do that in art. But not in life,
and I'm trying to be more "in life" these days.
I don't remember what I was thinking when I ripped the picture.
I think it was a version of what I was thinking while I taped it
back together. That there's a portal that opens in photographs,
and for a moment you're on the other side. Like imagining the distance
of the universe. Uncanny time. Diorama of ancient Rome.
Colorized, motion-corrected film of a walking tour through Paris, 1895.
The past has a present for you. How it felt,
watching fireworks all those years, thinking fireworks are death,
and then losing that, too, to the indistinct 9th of July. A Tuesday.

The Arborist

For a long time, I didn't know I was related to my mother. As family
secrets go, I think it's supposed to be the other way around,
like negotiating IN and OUT swinging doors, but families
are specifically themselves, the way the law is specifically itself.
Like a birth certificate. You can't change the place and time,
but you can change everything else, the law travelling us
to distant and unfamiliar lands and people, a madhouse novel,
puzzle-box science fiction, the narrative twist that my mother
is also my first cousin once removed. Dead now, and suddenly
my father, in his 90s, says to me that we were, before the adoption,
cousins or something, like he's helping, like he's remembering
a Get Out of Jail Free card.

                      Oh look! How did this get here?

Say the stories are true, and you die and step into Heaven.
Who greets you? That's the general idea, someone there
to say hi. And what do they call you? What essential,
true name you recognize in your very heart?
Go back three generations, and my great-grandparents
are the same great-grandparents, before or after the adoption,
waiting to greet me in death's airport terminal. They will say,
"Dear great-grandson" and the law won't object,
and the DNA won't object.
The theme is secrets. The theme is each new morning
absolves itself of last night's stars.

How about you? You've had a mouth full of clouds, too.
You've wanted to know things no one wants to tell you.
You've also touched the furniture of the dead.

Mouse Trap

There's no courage in saying things are a mess. Even now, as we make a table
to eat at. Remember the idea? Our sketching dolls voted yes.
The maps we made to move across voted yes, the way we wanted out of ourselves
and to be left alone, the way we wanted someone to belong to.
Family's the family you make votes yes. "Birth, school, work, death,"
as the Godfathers said, voting yes. I thought it was a great idea,
writing a book of poetry as if I were talking to you, asking us if we were happy,
and then never getting to an answer. It's because everyone agrees things
are a mess. Step two is the problem. Like how we have a problem with field mice,
so my winter job is mouse trapper. Find where they've been,
set the live trap, a translucent green box that looks like a little Monopoly house,
then take them to the dumpster at the industrial park, our frail small-town version
of an industrial park. Always the same dumpster.
That's an important step: keeping the family together.
This morning, mouse number two of the fall got out of the trap house
and was standing on the roof reaching up toward the covering of the trash can
I'd placed it in. The mouse looked like a child there,
wanting a parent to pick it up, and I had to maneuver it around at the dumpster
so as not to lose the trap. "Is this great literature yet?"
I asked the mouse, "The rising action, the conflict, resolution?"
Things are a mess, and sometimes, reading the great literature, I begin to feel
a kind of hope rising. I thought I was writing great literature once.
I was prepared for it. "That's not the great literature," Literature replied.
"In the great literature, we're at once the mouse and the idea of the mouse,
a hundred mice across the field voting yes." I'm thinking of the unified self
when I say things like "I was a different person then," how my greatest fear
was that I wouldn't be honest enough, or not making it true to living enough,
and then my greatest fear was that it would become tedious
and self-indulgent, voting yesyesyes, the relativity of all perspectives

and the transformation of all living things, from cell to creature to carcass.
I'm growing tired of ideas. We start our lives
as mailboxes. The next thing we know, we're the house.
We're in the house and of the house. And then we crawl to the roof.

As Quentin Tarantino's Torture Americana

Please, more love in our daily lives, we plead, but movie night
is for watching ourselves die. Happy endings are outdated
in an age of boiling tensions and red meat, so it's zombie love
lurching down the aisle. It's a kind of love, still, ritual sacrifice
spilling popcorn. Because going to work is too much, watching the news
is too much, we watch this creature rise from the ocean.

"Identity Issues, or Feeling Unsure of Where They 'Fit In'" is item three
on the Impact of Adoption list. It's how we can all feel adopted
on movie night, transactional. "Look at what I've done for you!"
the dead grandmother screams, transforming into a room of flames,
when a birthday card would've sufficed. Love tends to overreact,
make grand gestures. Natalie, at sixteen, loves these movies,
born just after the Twin Towers fell
in an apocalyptic rush, with a disintegration loop background
of thick gray streets and funerals. She did a report on it last year,
"Major Events in the Year You Were Born." You don't get to choose
your time, standing where you stand, sky of salt and ash.
Someone suffered here. The domino history of someones.
From their graves they call for air, their mute calling,
to have their true names spoken. Some jellyfish or trees
might as well be eternal in comparison. A child's in school,
hearing something in the walls, knocking. The father and mother
are replaced by empty space. We can't answer the questions
their ghosts raise from outside language and time.

My earliest memory of the Twin Towers is Philippe Petit, August 7,
1974, on a wire, a speck against the sky, dancing halfway

between, to, as he wrote, "etch his movements in the sky,
movements so still they leave no trace." I get it. I'm adopted.
Every time I say my name I'm half

                              way, and I don't look down.

"Adopt" as in "A Program"

You have to be careful not to fall in love with the spectacle. Spectacles
are easy. There's also the rest of the day to consider, as the torso
of Apollo shrugs, how old and broken things can create in one
a fondness for memes and tote bags. Something falls
from the sky. And we all know anything that falls from the sky
is a gift from the gods. Grape seeds. Bread. Lottery checks.
It's the premise of the Cargo cults dotted across the 20th Century,
deriving from the belief that ritualistic acts such as the building
of an airplane runway will result in the appearance of wealth.
It's logical conclusions from faulty premises.
                                             "The theme
of this year's Fall Harvest Ball is 'Fall Harvest'" proclaims the flyer
that fell from the bulletin board at the community center
as I passed. The theme is theme. We write it on our masks
and go running. We're exotic aliens to ourselves, asking,

                                             "Where is home
to you?"

The adopted child visited the Metropolitan Museum of Art
in 2008, wanting to get a little something to take back to the Midwest,
and their floor-wide installation turned out to be tractors. It's all
in how you define it, cult to denomination to nation, adopting
a program, adopting a pet, a child, from the Latin, *adoptio*,
from ad- "to" + optio "choosing." To choose. I'm dressed
in the best clothes I have. On a shelf, I'm Magilla Gorilla for sale.
I'm on a fact-finding mission to the center of my soul, working out
my family tree, birth + adoption = 2,000 people so far
                                             and still no mother.
I wish I believed in ghosts. Maybe I halfway believe in ghosts.

Magic Boat Ride

My adoptive mother's father died on Christmas Day, when she was three,
and my adoptive father told us it made Christmas hard for her.
She was *only three*, and how could we imagine that? It really got to him.
The holiday season, you throw your heart. Please send gifts. / Please
don't. When they adopted me, I was three. They had me call them
"New Mommy" and "New Daddy." Over time, the old life
falls away. Now, though, I feel I should say something. I think I know
how she felt. You're in a department store, and this song
keeps playing. It sounds like distant rain. Maybe an audience
shuffling. And look how colorful language is, like when one
"has a baby," we "had a baby," and then it's called "natural born,"
to distinguish it from being adopted, which makes the adopted, what?
"Unnatural born"? And we're told, no, it doesn't mean that,
you're overreacting, but when you're adopted, you do a lot of living
between denotation and connotation. My favorite scene
in *Willy Wonka* is the magic boat ride. Our blurred and secret projections
in a psychedelic slosh. My mother, waking for a Christmas
that will never come. Me, forgetting my name. If you can forget
your own name, you can forget anything. That's the part
that gets me. The *New York Times* ethicist is writing today
that the point of adoption is that your family identity
becomes that of your adoptive family. You are substituted.
You've been purchased and taken home, and don't need to wonder
where you were before. Should my mother have forgotten her father?
And so, what are the rules for each piece of candy one is offered?
I need to remind myself to ask that. You have this thing
you don't want to look at, so you look everywhere else,
and everyone sees this curious child, this brand-new outfit.

For example, the birth of a child to an adopted person, which may be the first experience with a biological family member, may cause the adopted person to revisit earlier issues of identity.

—Kohler, Grotevant, & McRoy, 2002.

I find a divorce record, Patricia Gorman and John Graff, 1978. I share it with Marie, who matches it with their son's ex-wife on Facebook. I message her. Some god flips a switch. The phone rings. "Hi, I'm Pat Gorman."

Because their relation to adoption has been associated with loss and even with stigma, adoptees and adoptive and birth parents have generally been, for the most part, isolated and fragmented in this aspect of their identity. (Thus, the versions of adoption that they have seen in literature may have been particularly important to them.)

—Marianne Novy, *Imagining Adoption: Essays on Literature and Culture*

Google search: "14 Amazing Movies about Adoption That Will Warm Your Heart." Feel-good story. Solution. Savior. *Pinocchio. The Dog Who Had Kittens.* Adopted into Royalty. Circus Brat. Doorstep Baby. Evil Orphan. Muggle Foster Parents. Replacement Goldfish. It goes on.

*flesh of my flesh

First Messenger

I find a picture of my birth mother online.

She's in her first year of high school. Centennial Union Yearbook, 1961.

You can already understand the nature of the hole. You look to the sky one night,

and there are so many stars, surely there must be life out there.

So you try telescopes, you try math, the habitable zone, presence of oxygen.

The dogs look up as the adopted child is hovering over sky charts

and birth announcements. "What," they say, "isn't this world enough for you?"

There are 133 stars within 50 light years from Earth visible with the naked eye.

It's probable there are Earth-like planets around some of them. We separate

the real and the unreal into two identical, unlabeled boxes.

We place them on a shelf in the garage.

                                        The story is searching for the story.

The problem with the story is empty sky. The problem with the story

is real. Who is your "real"? What is your "real"?

Once, I said, "Anything, for one picture." Now it's "Anything

for two." Stepping off

the back porch, looking up, I'm in outer space, forever

in every direction. Everything is superficial.

A mix of planetarium and dumpster-diving.

Like imagining 'Oumuamua would return.

That someone would be there. That we'd talk.

That we'd sit on the couch going through a shoebox of photos

spanning 6.5 light years to Hodge 301, the Pearl

Cluster, Jewel Box, Southern Pleiades, Andromeda.

I want to say. I want the clouds to say.

The mailboxes, in chorus, to say.

Hello from the Dumpster on Centennial and College Park

Last night I was sitting in the back row of the reunion of the dead
who hang on the family tree as empty spaces, a generation or two ago—
someone must remember—but they never got into
the pictures or stories, and I find two Patricia Gormans,
same age, sixty miles apart in 1961, Portland and Salem.
One is my birth mother. I'm homing in. We mark
by long strings of absence, the hands holding us we do not feel . . .
Sometimes, though, you find them, intentional

 or accident,
a reclamation project—

 here it is, like it was easy.
You just need the right number. Hello.
It's late afternoon on the west coast, and Pat Gorman is talking to me.
Which story is this one? Am I fixed
now? Is this what I needed? The way we say "great literature,"
and hesitate. Oh, memory, oh, dear
and delightful memory of sketches, of a bitterness

 more beautiful,
as the meaning of living is that someone will miss you when you're gone.

Later, I'm driving, a mouse in a translucent butterscotch livetrap next to me,
because mice stopped going into the translucent green one.
Therefore, it's different traps, but the same question.
How far away must one drive a mouse so that it won't return?

Cain went out from the presence of the LORD, and dwelt
in the land of Nod, on the east of Eden. So I go east,
two miles. That should be enough. Goodnight,
little creature. Good luck.

Garden of Mirrors

I look up from lunch and see a guy dozing back in his chair
and I imagine my dead father that way, perpetual sleeping passenger,
his head full of roads. "And who cares," he says in his dream,
"that since you'll never wake, that you're not inscribing memories?"
My odometer hit 123456 today and I had a minor celebration
and took a picture. Birds, scientists are saying, see the earth's magnetic field
as a kind of blue. I like that. I wonder if my father would've liked that,
as families have recurring themes, generation to generation.
Measure the shoulders. Measure a taste for parsley. Hand tremors.
As in the Enquists vs. the Gormans. The mother and father
are young, newly divorced. The Enquists want the baby, the child,
as he's three now, spring 1968, to be adopted out
through their side of the family to the Gallahers, and the Gormans
want to keep it in Portland, maybe cut a deal
over where it is and when. The Enquists sign the papers, though,
and the child is off on a Continental jet with a golden tail
to Kansas. (The painting that we're working on keeps folding,
fretting along the edges of the frame.) A few weeks later,
the Gormans are still not taking it well. For them, it was
a kidnapping. And one Gorman, the mother, goes off somewhere,
and the father, the Enquist, goes looking for her
with some friends. A friend of the father's, driving, falls asleep,
and down the hillside
into the trees. You fall asleep over this life, and you wake
in a doll playground in a doll town surrounded by a doll
forest. You're planning some sort of festival.
The Enquists and the Gormans understand each other,
as a desert understands rain. As now, 50 years later,
they've all gone but for the mother and the child,
and he finds her in late fall, and she asks him
if his eyes are still a beautiful steel blue.

43

Forbidden City

There's a Forbidden City within each of us. Unsharable maybe,
or unknown, some scrap of a television show or looking out
a car window, half-dozing, where I've had this vision all my life
of an ashtray. I've fantasized and fetishized this ashtray. It's a beanbag
ashtray, plaid, red and black, copper-colored metal insert
I could drive my finger around in circles. The kind with a monkey bars bridge
across the top to lay a cigarette on. From there
the room organizes itself: golden wood paneling, dark spots, inverse eyes
around a campfire. Then the film breaks, flipping and blinking.
Does it matter, in the end, if we're remembering this
or if we're imagining it? Yes, we swear, true life/this life/the one
and only life. Shake me, saint of memory, Saint Luke Baanabakintu,
we say. Shake me, panpsychism, tubes and wires, amnesia
and hope. One guards the image, because the image is fragile. The self,
the city, the nation unmoored. How one day, it's this telephone call
with my birth mother, 50 years 4 months 10 days later,
like we've been waiting for the golden anniversary to speak.

You rub a lamp on accident, and out springs a genie. A book falls
from the shelf, lands open to the code key. "Oh that!
That was my ashtray," she says. "The last time I saw you
was in their living room. I've hated knotty pine ever since."
It's the fall we hold because it's our fall. It blesses itself,
scattering around us. "This way to the egress!" P.T. Barnum
gives to childhood, as the spirits are dancing again, caught
in Renaissance poses. But sometimes the universe allows you an answer.
This happened. *I remember it.* Through everything. You whispered
to me. It's terribly important about the sun

                                        through the curtains,
how it catches the specks of the room hovering.

Night Life

I sit at the window, hoping to be found. / I sit at the window,
hoping I'm hiding. Pick one, both. And what we lose when someone dies
is a library fire, as the proverb goes. And we burn also,
browsing ashes, each unrecorded life
a Library of Alexandra, where between 40,000 and 400,000 scrolls disappeared
along with who shot JFK and the location of Cleopatra's tomb.
When looking for my birth mother, it would've been faster
to go to her childhood home, now a vacant lot with one maple,
and go door to door. She was five miles away,
working the desk at The Portlander Inn.
I might've stayed there while looking. I might've caught a show
at the onsite nightclub, The Ponderosa,
which has been doing Portland nightlife "Pondo Style" since 1969
featuring local, regional, and national talent.
I might've shown her these photos of two Patricia Gormans,
1961, freshman year Centennial high school, and 1962, sophomore year,
Salem high school. "Could these be the same woman?" I could ask.

We were talking on the phone last night about what it will be like
to meet. We're stressed. As Aristarchus of Samothrace, head librarian
of the Library of Alexandria, around 145 BC, got stressed
and exiled himself to Cyprus. Philosophy, Aristotle tells us, begins
in wonder, in a library, juggling torches.
I blink back to Howard Johnson's, over fried clams,
as my parents are telling me my father's dead. What was his name again?
"Roanoke?" They told my brother his birth mother was also dead, possibly
frozen in a hotel room. "She's living outside Seattle now,"
my birth mother tells me. "You know," she goes on,
"your father died with hardly a mark on him.

Just a small bruise on his temple. He visited me the day before, said he didn't feel well, and slept on the couch a few hours.

Do you think maybe some people just know?"

Leaving Elegy

This morning, I've the gym to myself. The music
is "Don't Stop Believing" which
is mildly embarrassing,
watching myself in the mirror.

Don't stop. Believing. Hold on to that dream. Yeah-ee-yeah.

As I'm leaving, a child says, "Love you love you love you,"
running across the child watch area
to her mother. I'm sure
I said it to my birth mother
in 1968, as I said it to my new parents later.

I must have, as any blank surface
one calls elegant.

The way one places one's hand
to a wall.
The way I placed my hand in yours.

The Many Worlds, Infinitely Saturated

> Sometimes it was as if I were in a dream and trying to perceive reality; then again I felt
>
> as if an invisible twin brother were walking beside me, the reverse of a shadow . . .
>
> —W.G. Sebold, *Austerlitz*

The coincidences. My birth mother was named Patricia, and
my adoptive mother, Kathleen Patricia. They both went by Pat.
When they adopted me, they renamed me John, while
my birth mother went on to have another son they named John.
It becomes a kind of hat. Something to add
to my hat collection. Like Jung's "synchronicity," or "Synchronicity"
by The Police, or the multiverse, with this replica world
in which I grew up as Eric, and the family calls me Marty.
I hate it. I call it a cartoon name. And Marty deals with it
or Eric does, with this anchor or sail
where they say names foretell your future, always adding up to infinity,
like a coastline. It's understandable.
We live at least three-quarters in fantasy. Or call it a lens.

I'm driving Eliot to school right now, in this life,
where I'm John. "Johnlife." There's this enclave
to the south of town we pass each morning. Near the entrance
is a spillway which, after heavy rain, swells with sewage.
The idea that the wealthy drive past the washed-up

                                       sewage of the town
to get to their enclave makes him laugh.

                        He prefers
to be called Boyd now. In the replica world, Eric sympathizes with that
in a JC Penny in Portland, where he's sitting
in the center of three fitting room mirrors, reflecting

a fan of Martys behind him, spread out
like gray-blue wings. Somewhere out there is a life
where no one calls me Marty. When I get out of this family, he thinks,
no one's ever going to call me Marty again.

The Poor Farm

70,000 years ago the human population fell to about 1,000.
There's some debate on this, but there's more genetic diversity
in chimpanzees who live 20 miles from each other than there is
in humans anywhere on the planet, A through Z. Hey cousin!
Hey. It starts to feel like faith, and how maybe my agnostic perch
is a color, not a form. That it's well and fine to stand
and sing, "I believe," as it's not the words or the notes,
but the singing that is us. Hello to 1946 glazed with rainwater.
Hello to 1971 which you were probably saving for breakfast. Hello
to 1965 is a rose is a rose is a rose. How long can we keep this up?
To say we're looking at it. And then to say I'm living with it.
That maybe I'm making a mistake, that it doesn't matter if we
keep this up or not, we're still keeping this up, as the commercial's on
again where this person walks through doors, each a portal
to another decade, another life-moment, school, work, love,
and back a little slower, with a bed of evocative, but upbeat, violins.
"Dear Concern," the scam email I just received opens, and yes,
that's it. Dear Concern, to each a dark night, believing it
important to the arc of yard mowing strategies, model airplanes,
woodworking experiments. It feels like it's leading up to something
but then it just keeps feeling that way, in languid indifference.
Hello to 1968 in a haze of lost connections. Hello to 1893, 1904,
rainbow rainbow rainbow. The hills are breathing, listen. It's 2001.
This matters if anything does. Hello from this room I'm in
at the Edgefield Hotel, where my biological grandfather died (brain
tumor, 1951) when it was the Multnomah Poor Farm. A light chill,

and I'm rocking in a replica of Chris Boyd's rocker, the unofficial greeter from 1931 to '63, trying to meditate into time travel.

*

I want to open a way of speaking that's absolute.

The Performance

Mother. Noun. My mother died piece by piece. It took
a decade. And now I get a replacement, going through adoption records.
"Better not fuck this up," I tell myself, because I think I'm funny,
which means I'm always apologizing and realizing I'm not so funny,
like how I walked into the dance studio just now
to say hi to Robin and Natalie before the high school football game,
and without taking the temperature of the room, which only
occurred to me to do later, I made some comment
about Natalie's dance makeup, which turns out to be
just the thing she and Robin had been stressing over for an hour,
because makeup, for halftime dancers, is ¾ of the world,
and I just blundered in with "Ew" or "Ugh." Funny dad,
look how funny I am, and so Natalie leaves saying, "I hate you"
and Robin won't talk to me. And I know this. What the fuck
is wrong with you, in this town, in this world, saying "ew"
about this makeup that she didn't want to wear in the first place,
but the dancers have to wear the makeup the theme committee
comes up with, and *The Incredibles* is stupid, of course it is, yes,
everyone knows that, but to say so is—*we must not say so*—
and why didn't I already know that, why do I continually
not know that? I'm trying to think here.

                                 Let me think.
I'm sitting in the stands with Robin. It's halftime. The dance team
takes the field, performs. Natalie has a trick where she
stiff-arm rolls forward and then flips over the backs of two
other dancers who lean forward. After, she comes up
to where we're sitting, to say hi, and she's all smiles.
"I usually slip the first time I do that trick," she says.

"And I didn't slip in practice, so I thought for sure I would then. But I didn't." And so everything is fine. Ha. Funny joke, this shape we take, as water takes shape, that we rise to and fill. As all the years there ever were are now.

Shame Experiment

By the 1840s, it was commonplace to warn against marrying
into a tainted lineage. The most common reason was lunacy, and asylums
were popping up like dandelions. The father has a history of insanity.
And here's the daughter, the grandson. Enter Gregor Mendel,
whose hybridization experiments on peas gave the practice
the level of abstraction it needed for respectability, but heredity was already
well-documented, part flea market, part horror show, as people
hoped to rid society of mental defects by catalogue. It's what
I'm reading this morning, about the about.

                              Census records
are released to the general public 72 years after Census Day.
1940 is released in 2012. 1950 in 2022. But after someone dies,
other records become available. Record of death, sometimes a cause.
It's a conversation adoptees are used to having with doctors:
"Is there a history of _____ in your family?" "Sure, why not."
To be adopted is to embody diaspora.

                              On other days, we're one
people, one in the spirit, from the one dust to which
we shall return. But in this context, like Census Day,
you're to check a box in a row of boxes. The acquiescence of time
is exhaustion. And so I've gone from having this one brother
I grew up with, also adopted, who at birth was my cousin,
(did I tell you that? I should probably make a chart).
to now having two more, and one's in jail, something about drugs
and alcohol. And I tell Robin, who has two brothers, one in jail
for drugs and money for drugs. I tell my adoptive father,
who had a brother die from alcohol, and my birth
mother, thirty years sober, tells me about my birth father's parents,
same story. My aunt Kate, Eric's wife,
tells me Eric was the only one who made it out OK.

"It got your aunt Luanna, too, your brother's mother."
We're a nonstop playlist, blaring from a runaway train.
And if you're going to think about these things,
at some point you're going to have to imagine God.

Encounter in the New World

Being adopted means I have options on "The Meaning of Your Name"
day. It was Enquist for a few years. "Juniper + twig." I was once
a twig of juniper. For more, I'm referred to "inquisitive"
and "exquisite" as something to hold or follow. My birth parents divorced
early on, so I might've reverted to her father's name, Gorman,
which is "dark blue," meaning "noble." Or maybe it's "spear"
and "protection," or maybe a triangular piece of land or a mountain.
It's about people to talk to, why we keep loving the future, passing
the time. We're clocks, as the time I broke my arm,
or got married, or lunch at Gray's truck stop, the future saying
there's a window and you might flicker by a triangular patch
of juniper on the mountainside where my birth mother, after I left,
married into the Graff family, and maybe I would've become that,
a quill, or pen. "Here's the deal," we say. Because everything floats off,
it's OK if we repeat ourselves. So I'm writing
of mountains of juniper under deep blue skies. It's how I say
I love this world. Your name abides. It carries you and follows you
like a shipwreck, the manifest, logs, and trinkets catalogued.
You have to do your business while you're here
because no one ever comes back. It's winter. My skin
is dry. I scratch it and bleed. I have red stripes down my legs
I don't remember making, that don't hurt, that I've never had
before. My thin skin. Newly thinned. And I want it to mean more
than wandering grocery aisles, reading ingredient lists,
preparation rituals, in the context of others, nation, neighborhood,
family, that maybe there's a core you somewhere,
and it's a rare jewel or maybe it's a mirror or just another surface,
a hollow sound coming from the Muzak system,
the kind of exhalation I remember from when my uncle died,
a Gallaher, which comes from "foreign help," or "one who loves

what's foreign," as I've been many lost things, we've all been
many lost things, the broken windows of the church, the stones
of the church scattered across the sleeping fields. It becomes
an idea, a kind of music. And names are the ruins of that place.

Friendly Ghost

Yesterday, I'm running down Munn, north to south, university
to high school, wide road, and an ambulance passes, lights
and sirens blazing. Later, circling back toward home, at the corner
on Munn and South, the ambulance pulls up all quiet now,
and stops. We make eye contact, me and the driver. It becomes
a philosophy: at some point you and the ambulance driver
make eye contact; until then, we file reports, have a sandwich.
Step one, on the Impact of Adoption list: "Struggles
with Low Self-Esteem." Step two, "Here are the people," we say,
gesturing to the family album, "and here's what they sang
at the campfire." The adopted child fills in the crossword puzzle
with sage and sandalwood. The adopted child moves through
101 levels of word scramble with an offering of fruit and dead bees.
It's like asking a glass of water what it thinks of the ocean.
The stories awaken. I tell my adoptive father that I found
my birth mother, keeping it general, light, because people say things
like "real father," "real mother," and "real" falters. "Let everything
happen to you. Beauty and terror. Just keep going," Rilke says.
In my earliest memory after the adoption, it's Halloween 1968.
I'm standing on the balcony dressed as Casper, the Friendly Ghost,
the ghost boy who inhabits a haunted house, with a community
of ghosts who delight in scaring the living. Casper, however,
is a nonconformist, preferring to make friends with people.
He packs up his belongings and goes out into the world. Takes up
running. You write the story of yourself, it's called *The Book
of Other People*. It's a theory of mercy, as life shifts you. Let's pretend
that's the theme, that we're characters, that the great literature
is talking, how the story shifted my great-great-grandfather,
by birth, James O'Gorman. He attempted suicide with a straight

razor in August 1880 on the tracks outside Careyville, Tennessee.
Found by the railroad bulls, he lived, made the local paper,
then disappeared, because there's also this other idea, the Right
to Be Forgotten, the Right to Erasure, Courtesy Vanishing.

The Movement of Crowds

When the circus comes to town, do you want to join or hide?
There are more options, but as on Election Day, this choice is binary.
Do you hear the train, see it on the horizon, or are you already on it,
boxcar open, your hair a swirl of options in the wind?
They say it wears you down, but I don't know, maybe you wear it
down, as the miles also make a music, a calliope. Last night, coyotes
started up, their high yipping in the field behind our house,
and our dogs barked back through the door, a world away.

What is unique? The adopted child is in august company
with the clowns, pondering their abstract concept, imaginary
as the past. So why not join the circus,
and call out "ALIENS!" on sketchy documentaries?
Close Encounters of the Third Kind is playing. The Third Kind is spiderlike
and slow, because that's the state of special effects in 1977,
and the question is, do you go with them, or just play the song?
This recurring idea that you've been placed here, you
and the pyramids, that you're E.T., and they might
come back for you. That you're really a secret agent, so secret
you didn't even know. Or you're the castaway, finally back
after years on an island, just you and your volleyball, and your life
moved on without you, unrecognizable now.
                                        It's not the world
that changes, just the lens, we say, looking through it, imagining
ourselves apart. And don't we all feel this way
at some point? I'm in a house. The roof leaks. Something's wrong
with the foundation. I go from window to window
constructing myself. As there's another option,
where the train comes to your house
and enters through the front door.

Blank Slate

When I meet my birth mother, I won't ask about the scar
on my forehead or the scar on my knee. One wants to empty
oneself, have it be forever a storm passed, the day clear.
"These children are blank slates . . . and if you adopt them . . .
they will become anything you wish," Georgia Tann
advertised, early 20th century. You go to the doll store. You go
to the robot store. I will make from the mud of the earth, an ideal.

She sold baby Ric Flair to a couple in Detroit. Maybe they saw the ad,
where "Little George" really wants to play catch, and is looking
for a mommy and daddy to complete his team.
Who could say no to that? It's the history of advertising in one panel.
Ric Flair's new parents decided March 18 would be his birthday.
That's a pretty solid day, generally, depending on where you are,
what you think about days, indoor party vs. outdoor party.

And yet, where did all these babies come from?
No one seemed to be asking. 5,000 stolen, and 500 or so killed
or left to die. Infamous adoption popularizer, child trafficker.
On my computer right now, Mary Tyler Moore is playing the part
of Georgia Tann in the film *Stolen Babies*, malevolent
and formidable, with coloring book dialogue and slow pans.

I'm the 24,641st person to watch this video. I'm EXT 1739.
I'm 1234 Chick Avenue. I'm Decree of Adoption NO. A18770.
I get it. Someone can wipe you away. Your name. History.
I can see dimly my forehead scar and the one on my knee, though
I can forget them for years. The bushes dance. We gift each other
flowers. And we don't ask some questions.

Elegy for the Gift Economy

I had this name on an envelope in the early 90s, "Pat Gorman,"
and a phone number. It came from my (also adopted) brother Richard's
birth sister, who'd hired someone to find her birth mother, but found us
and this name and number instead. I played cool. My brother's
meeting with his sister was a disaster. To even mention it
might push the family portrait from a picturesque view
into a boiling caldera. We entered the language of silence. But still,
my mother gives me the number. That's not nothing.
And when I call it, there's no Pat Gorman, wrong
number, another joke the universe plays, the universe
handing out free tickets to closed Broadway shows. But I still have
that piece of paper thirty years later. "If I'd've only done more,"
we say, when we find out later how close we were, the pebble
which starts the rocks which start the boulders which bring
down the Chaplinesque falling house,
dreaming a figure from the kitchen to the yard.

The gods change and the stars change into anyone the adopted child
is standing beside. Maybe we make eye contact at an airport,
any two people, hundreds of Patricia Gormans
whispering at once that a stranger gave birth to me,
a breeze across the final scene of Antonioni's *Blow-Up*
(1966), where a photographer who took a picture that seemed to reveal a murder
(which he then tries to solve, only to later give up) is walking aimlessly,
and comes across a group of mimes, two of whom are playing tennis,
invisible mime tennis, while the others watch. One of the players
hits the ball out of the court. Long arc. They all turn
to the photographer. He hesitates, then walks
to where it lands, picks it up, and throws it back. As the camera lingers
on his face we begin to hear a tennis match. You feel him
realizing this, almost bemused, almost wistful, as he turns away.

Alice Waking

It was a good thing, my birth mother and I are saying,
about the adoption. We're being positive. It's positivity day.
It's transformational tourism day. She was out of options,
and I was young enough to forget. As when one wakes from a dream,
in that moment one is still partially in the dream, knowing
this other world, even as the feeling dissipates. And yet, not
completely, so that a portal remains, and for the morning
one's full of thoughts of this other world,
as its perfume drapes the room,
like those moments we understand fully
we will die, the idea, that when you have it, tilts the room.
Then it softens, forgotten by lunch, but this feeling remains,
a chance that this door *leads*, that doors might *lead*.
Appearing as childhood. As misaligned parts some small thing jolts.

She found it difficult, never seeing me again.
On my way to the airport, she thought I looked so happy.
And I mention my stutter, how I couldn't pronounce *R* and *L*,
that it took years of speech therapy. "What do you mean?"
she says, "You spoke fine."

      History is a war of editors.

I walked in my sleep. They'd find me places, front porch, living room.
At night, at the window, I'd talk to a circling spaceship.
Sometimes it was aliens, astronauts, ghosts
in the walls. In *The Creation of the Humanoids* (1962), we're all
robots, reporting nightly to a central computer
called "father-mother." I've lost track

        of the hope or complaint,
though I've never felt more in a field. It's a question
disguised as Alice reaching for the doorknob,

the immensity of touch, reach,

as Alice grows larger then smaller. How the adopted child awakes

in the middle of a storm. How it's not this world and then it is.

The Second Idea of Absence

It smells like fall outside, mildew and chaff, what in Portuguese,
would be *saudade*, the presence of absence. As an approximation
it'll do, for when we're talking about things like fall, the idea
of some essential, some center, might as well be the smell of a leaf
you sat under once, years ago. It's like this new album I'm reading
a review of that describes it as having no relation to anything
going on right now, but says that it's good nevertheless, and I'm wondering
what it means to have a relation to anything going on right now.
Relate, mid-16th century: from Latin *relat-* "brought back."
The musical elements that relate RIGHT NOW, how we're talking
about anxiety, RIGHT NOW, the US president, an act of the mind,
how that makes the rest fall in line, contrapuntal
motion. But I'm thinking relation, how I had a son for less
than a year in 1985. His mother took him with her back
to Long Island, and I thought it was death, but it wasn't death. He's
34 now. Both facts equally a hole, and what do I say to him
about it? The heart's motor, elastic,

                                    into the sleeping century.
He takes a DNA test, and we share 3,465 cM across 69 segments.
He says hi after a year of silence. I'm hopeful. The album says, "Let's go."
I'd love to go somewhere, blast out into fall, shouting, "FALL!"
and have it be fall, a clarity of fall, unequivocally, unavoidably, removing
the masks from the Halloween party, and everyone's there, saying,
"I knew it was you, I knew it all along."

                                  "What is essential?"
droops, and wakes with a start, as there's always someone else
in the room who's never there. An absence that relates. The unknown
relation, from *referre* "bring back." It becomes travel. When I was 34,
I thought I was just starting. For a trip, you need comfortable shoes,
and in philosophy, we need mirrors. For a life, what's left?
It's like the journey to enlightenment, where, at first,

a mountain is a mountain, and then, during enlightenment, it's not a mountain, and finally, after enlightenment, it's a mountain. Each day is a realization, and each day it's the same realization.

We All Know That Something Is Eternal

I search "What to wear when meeting your birth mother," and the first result
is "Ways to Ruin an Adoption Reunion." So now I have this new thought
to occupy myself with. "Be interested," it says: favorite foods; favorite music;
what did they like to do in school; favorite place to vacation;
share pictures of yourself growing up.

In high school, junior year, I was George Gibbs in *Our Town*,
the 1938 metatheatrical three-act play by Thornton Wilder,
regarding small town Grover's Corners. I married Emily Webb,
who died during intermission
and ghost-watched us through the final act "Death
and Eternity." She asks the Stage Manager if anyone
truly understands the value of life, and he responds, "Not really."

The idea of the *Our Town* graveyard though, that's something
I get: the names in order, catalogued, the dead in their folding chairs,
neat rows, the Stage Manager wishing the audience a good night.

We botch so many things—whole lives, sometimes.
People should say "botch" more. It's a useful word,
so we don't have to say "fuck up" so often. That's what
I could say when I meet my birth mother. It will be a Monday, 3/25/19;
we'll be strangers in a restaurant who bear a resemblance,
and I will want nothing but to suddenly appear
in all the old family photos, birthdays,
4th of Julys, Christmases. I'm practicing each of them
in front of the bathroom mirror.

Haunted Oregon

Silence haunts the adopted child. I don't have a better way to say it.
So I fill my day with music. I fill my shelves with stuff from surplus.
I pick up rocks. And still, I'm enveloped in silence. I'm a letter.
I want you to write back. I want it to feel like a conversation. I want
ghosts. I want one of those Arcadia books, sepia-toned,
common typeface, boxes with space for a local picture
called *John Is Haunted and It's OK*. I want a complete set,
one for everyone I've known. *Haunted US*,
like the accreditation team haunting us this week
with their hard data and pursuit of truth. They meet with faculty, nod,
and are gone. "Were they here at all?" we might ask, as birds rise
from the trees, how my birth certificate reads "John Gallaher."
It's a legal truth, haunted by my ghost name, as official history
turns, so there's this buried thing one must search for,
dig up, if one wants to know, like how you come across vacant rooms
in the woods, especially by rivers. Once, I came across
a ruined shoebox of moldy photos. "I will carry this into the woods,"
someone thinks. Cans of beans and bits of clothing, cereal boxes, left
from our attempts at ordering the world.
I came across a car once, half-submerged in a river in Birmingham.
And the hotel I book for my "meet the birth family" trip, I find out
from my birth mother, was once the Multnomah County
Poor Farm, where her father died, and is on the list
of Oregon's Most Haunted Places, as you might expect
from an indigent hospital converted into a hotel, with turns
and doors to communal bathrooms, flickering bulbs, murals
of patients along the walls. Because truth is not beauty. "Hello,
shadow," one shadow says. "Hello, shadow," the other replies.

The Give Up Year

Just now I thought my coffee cup was empty, and that I'd have to go to the kitchen
to refill it, but when I picked it up, there was still some left, so now
I'm writing this instead of going to fill it. Now it's empty. Now I'm back
with a fresh cup. This is pretty much the way people would tell time
before 311 BCE, the Seleucid Era, when they began numbering years
rather than describing them by distinguishing events (The Year
of the Coffee Cup), local and unaligned

with outside forces.

It was difficult to imagine the future before 311 BCE—they didn't know
what to call it—and likewise difficult to conceptualize an end of time.
Numbers work much better. I drank a little coffee just then, thinking about it,
and then sat the cup back down onto a coaster I got from the Edgefield Hotel
where last week I met my birth mother, "2019: The Year
of Meeting My Birth Mother." In numbers, I can believe in 2029, 39, 49,
whether I'll be there or not, essential nature, walking
as ducks walk, a line of ducks, a series, until one duck says, "I give up."

"Is this

what you were looking for?" The Year of Meeting My Birth Mother asks.
But I've been looking so long, I've gotten used to it. Maybe I prefer
looking. It's all about approaches: compare /contrast, process analysis,
how this approach describes the walk, this other the walker.
The mother gives up the child. "Give up" we call it, The Year of Giving Up.
I give up. As if one is in battle, and surrenders. As if one has lost one's belief.
Give up. Surrender the child. I can go no further. I will give up
looking now, in this way, as she surrenders this picture of the two of us,
photo booth, 1967. She's 21. I'm two. Do we look like each other?
It's important we look like each other. Please tell me we look like each other.
I'm supposed to want more, and this is my failure. But
I've never seen a picture of myself at two. So close and foreign, *si près*—
awkwardly balanced on her knee. Here is my proof.

Maybe around the eyes? Chin? The Year of Balancing.

So we take our second picture, 52 years later.

"Sometimes you have to wait to get the light right," I say, Year

Zero.

Lucky Year.

Elegy for Brutalist Architecture

firmitas, utilitas, venustas

I have this picture my birth-mother gave me, or maybe it's birthmother,
or birth mother. Language is under pressure. It's a frozen lake
in late March you have to walk out on, 33 degrees, sun.
It's a picture of my grandmother, Tillie, standing with me
on her porch, right hand on my shoulder. I'm disappearing
into the folds of her housecoat. Bright

future. Heaven

of other places. The first principle of architecture
is earthquakes. It's the space
between any two things. And then you place a story
there. And then it's the space itself
you hold in your body. Blank of ice. You
and some other you. It's how I was reborn
or how I disappeared. How I blinked.

The second principle of architecture
is this booth we're in at the Edgefield Hotel restaurant, talking over
sandwiches and coffee. Story decorated. Attic
story, between "remember" and "forget." That on this porch
in 1968, Tillie has her right hand on my right shoulder.

It has to be invented. That in the third principle of architecture,
they bathe you and feed you. You won't remember.

And they know this.

Nest II

The bird's mother, thinking her egg will stay in the nest where she leaves it,
flies off to find food. But then the bird hatches. It doesn't know
where its mother is, so it goes to look for her. "Are you my mother?"
the hatchling asks the cat, the car. It asks a hen, a dog,
a cow, before widening out to a boat and a plane,
as well as a power shovel which lifts it back to its nest
just as its mother returns. The two are reunited, much to their delight,
and the hatchling recounts the adventures it had

                                     looking for her.

Maybe you've seen this book
(written and illustrated by P. D. Eastman, 1960): aqua cover with the hatchling
standing on top of a sleepy-looking hound's head. It was
my favorite book, the part with the power shovel especially,
and my adoptive mother would read it to me. I've no idea
what she was thinking, or what I was thinking.

I'm walking a tightrope, a note

                            passed from a scared girl
to a model village. Along the way, I lost track of myself,
and had to be brought back, clumsy, dazed,
to meet my birth mother again. In a parking lot,
half a century later, we have to pick each other out of a crowd.
I want to say we're not strangers. That there's some switch
that gets flipped. But there's no switch. We have lunch.
This isn't joy.

          (Something else.) Pictures
at Multnomah Falls with Dan, my brand-new
half-brother Dan. Ice cream. I buy a hat. Green background.
It's a fundamental question, "Are you my mother?" One would think
Yes or No. But it's not that easy. It goes like this:

at the Portland airport, waiting for my plane,

across the concourse, I see myself, framed

by the blue and green carpet. I'm three. It's 1968.

And all the things I've covered my life with have torn away.

Building the Cathedral

The anonymous builders of English medieval cathedrals,
26 cathedrals in 500 years, would rarely see the end of the construction.
It was unhappy work, and the Church
helped recruit laborers by granting indulgences. Indulge me, Lord.
Grant me pardon as I lift this rock. I was clumsy and raw,
placing my hands to the cold stone.

Portland in March, and I'm driving with my brand-new
just-found half brother, Dan, to meet our second cousin
Ken.
  "Bonus family," the new language
calls us. "This is the road your dad died on," he says.

I've found my birth mother, and this is the transformation,
brick by brick. I say it aspirationally, that every stone
is the corner stone. The cathedral
of the body, the history of the body. Ken
says hi. We're all five foot seven. The three of us
in an arc. We have lunch.

The next day, I flip through the Troutdale historical records looking for my biological
great-grandfather, the one-time mayor. I run
in the golf course behind the hotel. My rental car is $39.99 per day.

Hewn, as in "hew to the line," "stick to a course," literally,
seemingly contradicts the sense of the verb, *hew*,
to "cut evenly with a weapon or tool." The stone
is hewn. I'm listening to an album by Big Thief.
I'm thinking about running another loop. Then I fly home.

Cleave, as in "to split or sever, especially along a natural line." Then
cleave to, to stay close. Watch these graves
dotting the hillside, buoys on a slow-motion rough sea.

For the Dead Mothers in Disney Movies

Unity is also a kind of scab, as the old minutes are replaced
by the new minutes. The adoptive mother dies
and joins the birth mother
in the realm of the imagination, and then the adopted child
finds the birth mother
and she joins the adoptive mother
                                    in the photo album.

Today my odometer hit 124816 and it means things
are doubling up. When I met my birth mother, as a gift,
she gave me a pair of fingerless gloves she knitted. They're handy
(nice joke, she says) in my cold office.
I'm afraid to wash them. The knitting seems fragile.
They look like they're barely holding on.

I'm trying to think.

Natalie's upstairs in a foul mood, slamming doors. But then,
fifteen minutes later, she's all humming, just fine, so who knows
the relationship teenage daughters have with doors.

Like the mysterious accents that come and go
in low-budget films, I know something is happening,
but what? As if it's the room itself that's the point, the butterfly
lifts off, wobbles, as a form of answering, or floaty
in a typhoon, inside you there, me here, is one. But that's not it either.

It's how you want someone next to you to see something far off,
so you point, only they can't follow your line of sight—we're quite

bad at that, trying to move our perspective a bit to the side—
and you both fail, until they, with a hint of frustration maybe,
land their gaze randomly on whatever, and say, "yes, yes,

I see it now."

All the Young Mothers of 1911 Agree

Is it time to say "quit" or time to say "just getting started,"
when you're making your family tree and end up at the 1564
wedding and Baumstamm Sagen of Wolff Mornhinweg
and Ursula? They're the first scraps of my DNA, among thousands
of scraps. Ursula, meaning "little bear," was popular
in the middle ages. The wedding was fabulous. Standing
on the X. YOU ARE HERE, begin, like looking at the earth
from space, or putting sheets on the bed, dryer fresh,
whispering "zero." Further back, across the continent,
there was a competition held each year for over 300 years, a minimum
of three plays per playwright per year. Fragments of the list
remain, a few plays. After the show, we sit in the field
with our sandwich, dance trophies, soccer trophies, like a breeze
blowing gently over the sea. The cabinet opens
and spills through time, the twisting strands
that mark us, that tie me to this picture Gary sends of his mother
at four and my grandfather at a few months, with their parents,
the Enquists, proud in front of their fishwheel,
1911, where Bonneville Dam is now.

                                     Last night, the Maryville girls'
high school soccer team played Chillicothe. 3-0. Good win
in a difficult season. Just before the half, Natalie took
a hard hit on her weak ankle, and during the break, Dale, the coach,
taped it, stirrup and anchor, just like in the videos,
and she went back in. There's an empty box somewhere
in which the past is dreaming of us on their afternoon walks
around Bonneville Dam, that no incantation lifts
from this photograph they also held, located now
at the Troutdale Historical Society. We sit awhile longer in the grass,
play 250. My favorite play so far, we say, maybe, or, the school lunch account
is getting low. I'll send you with some money tomorrow. OK.

To Be Happy, They Suggest

you get to a place of forgiveness. It's New Year's Eve. The countdown
is on. Skiff of snow over the town. A single engine turbo prop
flies over. I used to fly around in those planes with my dad
and I kind of miss it. The new research is telling us that
you're to write your story twice. Maybe four times would be even better.
Six, infinity. Maybe we'll be able to forgive our chairs
and beds by then. Our flowers and sidewalks. Like poor choices
for side items on a cheap menu. To forgive, one must look
at oneself twice, to go through the photos, forgiving each one,
starting with the frame. The idea is to move on, get to "a place,"
as if one might travel there, this town full of people on a pilgrimage,
a vacation spot, where maybe you end up with a job at a gift shop.
Or else you're having to share the parking lot with all these
out-of-state plates, ducking their epiphanies: "Here we were,
thinking we were helping," or "Here we were, envisioning things
going a different way," or "Something worse might've happened."
OK, then. It's a complex city map, every city over the top
of every city. It's Karaoke Night at the Flying J. Out-of-date
living room decor. A shoe store of used shoes. In my real town,
I live against one of the main roads out. A siren just went past.
A lot of forgiveness travels that road. I've travelled that road
holding my breath, burning incense for my adoption records.
My birth mother says, "OK, ask me anything." And I don't
ask anything. It's moving day. My dad feels bad now about
the way they handled the adoption. He's not specific, in the way
forgiveness is a general direction. Go south past the amusement park,
you can't miss it. Forgive us our directions. My birth mother
phrases things differently. We all phrase things differently.
Christmas Day, I called them both. I said, "Merry Christmas." Hey,

I get it. There are a lot of people I could call. "Hey, hi, I
forgive you, and/or please forgive me." And they could reply,
"Excuse me, I'm sorry, who are you again?" I'm new here
at the gift shop. It's a new year. I'm saying "happy" everywhere I go.

Loss is a central theme to adoption, and it is experienced by all constellation members.
—childwelfare.gov

The ghosts who trail everyone in the adoption triad make up a shadow cast of characters. . . These ghosts are too dangerous to be allowed into consciousness. Instead they are dissociated, consigned to a spectral place I call the Ghost Kingdom. It is not located on a map, but in the geography of the mind.
—Betty Jean Lifton, "Ghosts in the Adopted Family"

"Forever Family."

The adopted, and their natural and adopted parents, must themselves come to a solution without benefit of a general understanding. Let them look away from their paralyzing silences and their secrets and see whether speech has something to offer them . . .
—Jean Paton, *The Adopted Break Silence*

In the ancestry commercial, all ancestry is meaningful. My results read 30% Scotch-Irish, 26% Finnish, 24% Swedish, and 20% across eastern Europe. I go back months later, and my history shifts: 28% Finland, 26% Ireland, 18% Germanic Europe, 19% Sweden-Denmark-Norway, etc. I get a kilt, the ad goes on, and the bagpipes play, or I can call myself "Erick, the Angry Finn."

The cousin chart.

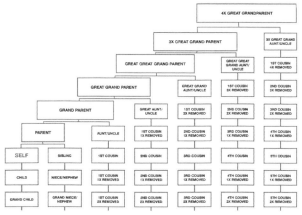

https://genealogy.org.nz/Forms--Charts/11155/

*kin of my kin

Un-

Unanswerable questions that kind of hurt to even imagine answering
or because they're unanswerable in the first place:
what was your father thinking when he died? That kind of question.
He was asleep when the car flipped, so maybe he was dreaming.
Dreaming and then stepping through a door.
                                                        Part of you
wants to think of this as a beautiful way to go, and the rest of you
says dying takes place as a rock thrown into a pond,
and we can debate the size of the rock, or trace the angle of the throw,
calculating the path of waves or particles through regions
of varying propagation velocity, absorption characteristics,
reflecting surfaces, but bordering each pond, there's a sidewalk
leading from A to B, where someone's pushing a stroller
containing a little dog, thinking about what some cloud
looks like. They're not thinking "what are they doing over there?"
How suddenly you're interested in the spiritual realm,
and continue that way the rest of your life, or you get into collecting
bar signs, or automotive-related items, because you can't keep
throwing rocks and crying. Or you keep throwing rocks and crying,
because now you're a pro at that. A debt that circles,
that you prune, make into a shrine, the shrine of your debt,
like a credit card, a little drawer of saved credit cards
you neither forget about nor remember, that simply remain.

*

And then my DNA-testing fad ends, 02/02/2020, a palindrome day,
which tend to cluster at the beginnings of each millennium.
The next will be December 2, 2021. Twelve people
were killed last night outside Los Angeles. Someone today
is making calls to family, preparing the memorial services, ripples

tearing through their lives, as my neighbor, whose husband
is back from the hospital after falling two nights ago,
is stepping from her front porch for the paper,
hunting around for it in the early blue cold of February.

The World as Itself

Our neighbors are gone. They moved to Kansas City
where they've family who can help after the husband's stroke.
He was festive on his last walk last night, said we'd been good neighbors.
But I couldn't remember his name, and I didn't want to ask, not
now, after he said something like that. Nod and smile.
A family with a teenager is moving in, same age as Boyd.
Everyone you know is gone, click, with their memory
and houses and streets. Stand here long enough, you'll see it flinch.
Our yard's doing that. Years ago there was a drop-off,
now it's smoothing out, easier to mow, as the future slips
out of sight past our neighbor's ornamental rock garden. Everyone's
on edge. I've stopped going to the ancestry website,
and the ancestry website wants me back. "You have hints," it says.
A new cousin! Updates on your birth mother! But I don't go back.
Here's the picture of my birth mother I waited 50 years for.
Stare at it long enough and you can see it flinch. It's been almost a year
since we've talked. Distance is my jam. "The more we tried
to make it feel like home, the less it felt like home," the mannequins say,
propped in our chairs along the porch. They're listening
to the radio, and making long-distance calls to 1984 when malls
were everything. We couldn't imagine our lives without malls.
Now, mannequins are mostly unemployed, but even in that,
they're stand-ins for us, in our best proportions, because we
don't know what to make of ourselves otherwise. They sit
on our couches reading the great literature. Then it's "How much DNA
do we have to share before we can call each other cousin?" The new
thinking is that the universe isn't shaped like a balloon, but like
a donut. On the bright side, it's still a party! Boyd laughs at that. Ha.
We watched our friends' dogs last week. There's a cardinal
which keeps trying to make its nest in the wreath on their front door.

It would seem a smart plan. Out of the wind. Nice arch. But
it's a flurry of chaos when we turn the corner to their door. It's how
one dreams of making a life. The corbels and fences, crisp lawns.

Lugubrious Salutations

I'm driving past the empty soccer field, saying, "football pitch."
The mouse that's riding beside me in the translucent green live trap
rolls its eyes. I get that. I'm rolling my eyes, too. Yesterday
I was cruising the aisles of Hy-Vee for charcoal toothpaste,
and I don't know why. It came over me in a wave,
like when I first understood how to tell time. Now it's easy
as "hello" and "goodbye," and antique candy is calling to me
from boutique shops in tourist towns in Colorado.
I'm listening so hard, people, that the sky turns a pale pink,
like when I was six in speech therapy, repeating sentences
into a mirror, a little Narcissus of propriety, getting all fixed up,
placing weather balloons across the Mayfair set.

I have a voice now, indistinguishable from TV news,
though I don't know much about weather balloons
outside of press releases after UFO sightings, but I can guess,
as the speech therapist had to guess at my speech and/or language
disorder, as I'm also guessing what the Mayfair set is, as the mouse
is guessing. And then we're to the dumpster, and I realize it's empty
but for several inches of water. That would be a rough end
for the mouse, so I put it into a nearby trash can instead, full
of McDonald's bags, and I feel OK about how this is going.
I hope the mouse does, too. I really mean that. It's a nice day. 76
degrees. A lot of McDonald's bags to explore. These are life and death
decisions, like last week in Colorado, when I hopped onto a rock
so Boyd could take my picture, and I put my left hand to the cliff face,
and off falls this chunk that strikes me in the leg, just below
the knee, because I can't jump or anything, not knowing if jumping
would be worse, so I have to take it, and then
                                          I feel the blood,

and Boyd says, "OK, got it." And here I am.
I'm shaking this translucent green live trap
like it's a stubborn can of parmesan cheese,
the mouse holding on. Cloudless, the sun already warm.

Echoes of a Theme by Brutalist Architecture

Saint William of Perth who died circa 1201, also known as
Saint William of Rochester, because why limit yourself,
is the patron saint of adopted children. I like that, someone
to intercede, so that things aren't just against you, and the adopted child
could use that, only in this story the child
Saint William adopts goes on to murder him.

                                          And here we are,
in the Brutalist architecture of courts and clerks,
as a formal address to God in God's language of silence,
in which God never stops speaking.
The way the frame is an answer to where you stand, who you are,
or seeing is an act of imagination, these long strings
of chopped-up philosophy.

And so here's Loki, trickster god, cast as Thor's adopted brother in the movies,
with his hodgepodge outfits and crooked crown. To even think it,
I'm sorry. I should be thinking
all different things. The adopted child grows up
saying "I'm sorry" and "thank you."

Dear Saint William of Perth and Rochester, I'm feeling ungrateful
this morning, 2:27 a.m. unable to sleep. We are all trembling light.
The survival story, the love story, the mystery story,
the transformation story, the creation story. The story
that breathing tells. I wanted too badly to leave nothing out
and now look at this mess,

                         sprawled across my life of omissions.

Jury Day

I'm called up for jury duty. It's weird how things go. The prosecution
introduces the case, a quick overview. They will show a history
of abusive behavior, culminating in a scene
in a grocery store. Then a response from the defense.
We're allowed to ask questions, and so it seems a good time
to ask one, when the defense gives us a knowing look,
and says, "Who hasn't at one time or other gotten frustrated
with our kids?" Because, you know, the defendant
isn't being charged with frustration, so I ask about that,
because when one is adopted—I think such thoughts, scenes.
And the next thing I know, I'm heading home. That's the story
of my day in the jury pool. This morning, I was standing
by the bathroom door, and gave my shirt an underhand throw, lateral
to the hamper, ten feet away, and *woosh*. I make fantastic shots
when no one's looking. That's frustrating. And at the mall
last Christmas, at the chocolate shop, they came around
with the sample tray as if life is free. But they're not fooling anyone.
Which is frustrating. And frustration is a hallmark of comedy.
We get to watch ourselves as wacky clowns in a blur
of holiday mishaps. I read the paper for weeks
after my jury pool morning. Nothing. It's as if the day never existed.
Or the paper, even, as it's a small town paper
that's disappearing in my hands. It was all some dream
where reporters are waiting for me in the hall. They have pictures
of crying children. They say, "Look at the children,"
but each of them is a picture of me when I was a child,
and the face in the picture is moving: tilt down, tilt up, slight twitch
of the mouth, eyes not quite tracking together, but pretty close.
I have a lazy eye, the reporters inform me, and they've been following it
for years. They want a statement. Have you been listening to Mars
lately? What does Mars have to say? The newest end of the world

is that oxygen will be gone in a billion years, starting now.
So I hold my breath. I've a billion years to practice. Like passing
a graveyard, I pass the courthouse every day on my way
to work. Snow, flowers, rain, sun. Every day.

The Idea of Community

In the cartoon version, the protagonist is left in charge of a baby
who is in some fashion courting disaster. It's accident-prone. It's a maniac.
And the little creature's delivered, last second, back safe
like nothing's happened. Perhaps the protagonist, by this time,
is heavily bandaged or smoldering, Tom & Jerry version, Daffy Duck
version. In the Chick Avenue version,
I put the dogs out to run, and hear a parent bird going crazy
before I see what's going on. A little bird, not yet able to fly,
is in Daisy's mouth. I do the "make-angry-face-
and-shout-DROP-IT" routine, and Daisy drops it, flopping
and spinning in the grass. I shoo the dogs into the house,
and go to see to the bird. I hate days like this.

I'm trying to be positive about life cycles. My father's in his 90s,
declining. It's God's machinery, but what exactly
am I supposed to do with some flopping, mostly dead thing?
It turns out though, that the bird isn't dead. A bit of a limp, but otherwise,
looking steady-ish. Except it can't stay in the yard. This
is the dog yard. The parent bird is still going nuts above us.
It's a standoff. And I'm not convinced that evolution has done a good job
with birds. My father called the other night. Actually, I called him,
but halfway through the conversation, he said

the reason he called me
was to find out how things are going, and I didn't correct him.
That's how things are going. The nest is twenty feet up. That's also
how things are going. So the best I can do is usher the bird
to the other side of our fence. I'm helping things along. Here you go,
little bird, on your way. And the thing about cartoons
is that even in cartoons

death intrudes with bigger and bigger fish,
in sequence, emergent phenomena swallowing each other.

Baby birds don't know these things. Parent birds aren't equipped, so before I'm even into the house, the little bird is into the road. Busy road. And then it's a car, just like that. 35 mph. And the parent bird is no longer carrying on and the day grows quiet.

Bio Lab

An experiment on bacteria has been running for over 30 years, every day
in the freezer and test tubes, 70,000 generations and counting.
It's an evolution experiment, looking across the chasm, a glimpse
into the whirlwind. We do these things: the great American novel;
award season; a cargo ship of luxury cars on fire and adrift in the middle
of the Atlantic. Pick 1910. The life expectancy of a female was 49 years,
nine months, then, and 48 years, three months for a male. The experiment
is any shoebox of undated black and white photos. The news
tells me that redwoods nurture each other, and the next question is
if they're thinking about it, then "what is thinking?"

7,500 generations of anatomically modern humans later,
here's the only extant picture of Robert Gorman, 1910, at 6 months.
He makes it three more years. Here's his sister Shelah, three,
who makes it another seven. Robert dies when his clothes catch fire
as the kids are burning leaves, and Shelah from a .22 rifle with a jammed shell
that a brother and neighbor kid are trying to remove with a pocket knife.
Redwoods are passing distress signals through a network
of mycorrhizal fungi. The season's dry. A technician in the lab
turns out the lights for the night. "Enough with this long, drawn-out
panic attack," she says, packing up the simulation universe.
People will burn their pictures if they get cold enough.
People will eat the temple if they get hungry enough. Dear history,
dear contingency, I'm having a sudden intensification of feeling,
tabulating possibilities and predictions. I was changing a tire
in front of the house, 1999, and the jack gave way
into the heat of the tarmac. The car fell. I rolled out, the steel mounting
glazing my shoulder. How petty have been my desires. Dear history,
on the way home from Kansas City tonight, early March,
Boyd and I are in the rain, then through a veil, to a sudden snow, whiteout,

all ice, and the Mazda fishtails, 60 mph, three lanes. I'm blank. We're
silence. We're a set of functions. My first father, who died
this way. And then we're through. And we see ourselves again.

Battleforce Arpeggio (I-35)

I'm going to try today, even though there is no TRY, there is either DO
or DON'T DO. *Star Wars* told me that when I was a kid.
Fuck *Star Wars*. That's a terrible philosophy. I'm sticking with "try,"
because I'm driving to see my dad in hospice and "try"
feels like it's the size of Mars right now.
I'm pretending I'm Grace Paley, writing, "A Conversation with My Father."
I'm pretending I'm driving to my father's final illness.
I'm pretending I'm driving to my father's funeral.
I hesitated. I didn't start driving after work. Instead,
I went to my son's soccer game. Listen, friends,
the game was so perfect, I thought I'd died and this was some sort
of goodbye fantasy. I'm pretending I'm dead. So now
I can talk to the ocean as well as the stars.
And I'm going 83 mph and I have 35 eyes.
I'm pretending I'm talking with each of them.
The earth tilts and we call it seasons.
It's hard to win the Nobel Prize, and yet someone does it every year.
Nothing's more dangerous than a curious angel.
I don't believe in angels, so that's easy for me to say.
I'm pretending I'm writing a sitcom called "Hanging Out with My Father as
   He's Dying." "Yeah," I say, "everyone's always complaining about my place,
   too. How I don't keep it clean enough, acting like they've never seen blood
   before."
It's more a conceptual show, like saying to the Nobel Prize winner, "Hey,
remember back when you were innovative?"
I'm pretending I'm a bitter two-bit comedian on the lam from God,
which I'm trying to phrase into a "Lamb of God" joke
and then giving up. That's the two-bit part.
Dying on the tier system. Dying by plateaus.

I'm pretending we're talking about slope farming.

It's the terrace cultivation of death. Why am I suddenly so thirsty?

It's like someone forgot to invent water.

Drought. In which I go through the seven emotions on I-35 from Oklahoma
City to San Antonio listening to *Automatic for the People*.

Hey, Texans, whatever your reasons are for living here are not good enough
reasons to deal with this traffic.

I tell him that when I get there, 4017 Cypress Court.

It used to be in Cibolo, but now they say it's Schertz.

So, OK, whatever. Life is change. Everything resolves.

There's nothing that can save my father. He's not even

in any pain. I'm pretending I'm telling him it's now considered healthy

to drink two cups of coffee a day. I'm imagining my car

is a confessional booth:

It has been many miles since my last confession. Bless me.

When I get there, I ask him what he's been thinking about, because what do
you say to someone who's dying?

Do you dream of stopwatches?

I've been dreaming of stopwatches. It's stopwatches everywhere. It's like we're
trapped in a referee supply company.

Before I left the house, I rigged up the wind chime with paper clips and an old
padlock for the weight.

And how's your masterpiece going?

Change is everything. That's what the Salvation Army says

every Christmas. I call my kids and tell them that.

What's the most important thing you learned from a parent or guardian?

My father would blow up when I'd add something like "or guardian"

because he believes there's only one way to do things.

It was difficult living with him

and I'm glad I don't do it anymore. Thinking that

makes me feel like I'm wishing he was dead

and I'm not. I tell him about the coffee. I'm pretending he answers,

because he's currently asleep.

I'm pretending we're having a conversation.

I've been pretending that many years.

The worst phrase ever invented is "Happy Hour."

Outside, it's a blood red sliver moon.

If I just keep adding more stuff here

he doesn't die and I don't die and no one dies and wouldn't that be great.

Someday, it's the same answer for every question.

There's nothing up my sleeve.

I'm pretending that if the devil is six, and God is seven, then the universe is
    eight, lying on its side.

It's like we're always told. In mourning, I will cut my hair

and my hair will continue to grow.

I will shave my head, and my hair will continue to grow.

I will sweep the floor. I will sweep it again.

I'm pretending my father is alive.

Driving back, the directions say, "In three miles, take a left

on Purgatory." I'm pretending my GPS is making a joke

as the landscape spreads out over itself in every direction.

Nest III

This morning, like most, I'm up before dawn, at the window
as the road and field across the street slowly appear. A truck rattles past,
headlights on, the last few minutes of dark. I'm up
because Natalie's up, 5:15, for dance before school, three weeks
from turning 17. The ritual, one year from being over, is this: one Eggo, light
spread of peanut butter, syrup, cut in squares. Then lunch: peanut butter
and jelly sandwich, a fruit (her favorite's pineapple), some gummy fruit
snacks, and whatever little crackers we have (Goldfish, Ritz). Then it's her
filtered water in the Hydro Flask, because we don't trust the city water. 5:50
she's gone.
At some point in this, I turn on my computer and make coffee. Flip on some
music,
quietly, and maybe quote from what's playing as a good-bye. This morning, it's
"Can you hear me now, ghost?" And she says, "OK, bye."
6:20, and it starts again with Eliot. He's hard to wake up.
I have to bring the Eggos to his bed and stand there
until he starts eating so he'll not fall back asleep. But once awake,
he'll start talking, some scrap of a dream or thought. This morning,
it's "We were just running, weren't we?" Yeah, we were. And now
that was four years ago. Natalie moved away, and he's a month from 17.

Narcissus fell in love with his reflection, and gazed so long he disappeared
in the feedback loop. You live by the image /
you die by the image. "Why am I sharing this with you?" Narcissus
is unable to ask, enthralled. But Narcissus is the story, even so
over one's phone or scrapbook or diary. It's the solace of description,
as in the 1800s, when one would lay one's diary on the sitting room table
for people to browse. They'd mail them back and forth. Here,
we say / they said. *Here*: "I guess you will take
a good laugh at this picture when you see it," Tillie writes, summer 1922.
You can trace the loops of "good," feel the living hand move

along the page. "Tillie writes," you can say. She's anyone.

She's in the other room as I'm looking out

over the road. The field falls in love

with the map. And I'm trying to be more of a day-to-day person,

not looking too far ahead

or behind. Define "too far." Or better, don't.

From the Map of the Folded World

Lichens can survive in space, I'm reading, and I feel a wave
of kinship with lichen, so I look them up, as I'm not all that confident
I know what they are. Turns out they're composite organisms
in a mutualistic relationship, and I feel a metaphor coming on,
which I resist. It's important to resist metaphors when you feel them
coming on, or you might end up on a motivational poster
in a workstation, some manic pluralism that collapses to homogeneity.
These relationships are also a problem in outer space, as the bacteria in our gut
change there, and that could be a mutualistic big problem—or
who knows—maybe not a problem at all. Maybe the trillions
of bacteria traveling with us would love the change. It's like saying,
"I'm reading this poem right now." The reality is more complex.
Or like saying, "I like marshmallows because death." I like
a lot of things because death. In fact, liking things is only possible
because death. But I'm not going to thank death for it.
                                                        So I'll live
like that. Then the great literature steps in to say nothing
is permanent, and disappears.

*

We evolved to be lonely, the thinking goes, in order
to keep us together. My birth mother lives by herself,
and reads and keeps the TV on.

We say we're ready for the mountain.
Look at all this stuff.
But we're not ready for the mountain.

When you get there, you realize
you've never seen a mountain before.
You've never been this alone.

Clerical Error

It's my birth mother's birthday, and I want to say hi,
but I don't want to end up in a conversation. I imagine
she feels the same, that we're *alike*
in that way. So I text my half brother Dan for her cell,
and he forwards her contact and it comes in as MOMS CELL,
replacing my mother's number who died years ago,
and now everything's weird, but also funny. Maybe not funny,
I don't know. The tools you use determine what you find.
Is this who I am now? Tonight, I'm going to try "conscious sleep"
that I just heard about on the radio on the way to the grocery,
because most days seem a kind of "unconscious awake."
Maybe this will balance things out. I'm at a flea market
talking with the fleas, how everyone who died, instead,
maybe someone else died, until I turn,

and it's the DMV, and they're congratulating me on passing
my vision test without my glasses. Wait, when did I start wearing glasses?
They're saying reality is an illusion the mind creates, so flip
a coin, as one can feel exiled, adrift, but maybe land at a place
much better than where they came from. Like the happy
adoption story, or anything you've been through, so I'll say, "exile,"
call everything exile, as the pope has declared
St. Joseph, the adoptive father of Jesus, the "protector
of exiles." Jesus, then, an exile. And like the kicked-out Jesus,
I'm in exile, like my birth was Waterloo, and I'm wandering
the grocery aisles of Elba tonight, our myriad duties,
like my shadow in the parking lot splitting four ways under the lights.

Caveat

Things aren't going well with my dad. He's frail and telling
the home hospice people that he wants to go to a nursing home.
He's mad about the food the neighbor brings over. What even is this?
Who would eat this? So, the social worker calls me, because
when the patient does this long enough, it's everyone's shot nerves.
We go back and forth and come up with a plan,
that he could go into a nursing home for five days,
called "respite care." And after that, maybe he'll decide which
he likes better. So, I call him, ready with The Plan,
and it turns out my cousin Margaret is there from CA. She has
a background in elder care and she's decided to stay
the rest of the year. He's ecstatic, and says he's so happy a "blood
relative" is there for him. Since my brother and I are adopted,
I pause a moment. Language isn't neutral. It's just

that he's so happy . . . I tell her he can be a handful.
She says she's up for it, as she's between jobs anyway
and wants to move to TX, so this lets her check the place out.
There's not really a lot to check out from my dad's house, but sure,
if you're good, I'm good. Things go OK, then not so OK,
then OK again, and he talks to another cousin, Anne,
who's a lawyer, and he says he wants to adopt Margaret.
Margaret calls to say sorry about that. He's her uncle,
that's enough. Anne says he's not really going to do it.
He's just in that stage. I'm not much for conclusions. I prefer the shapes
of shadows and music, which I move through riding my bike
across the university's campus, so many connected parking lots.
They seem to go on forever. And just like that, my father dies
one October evening while I'm at the grocery store.

Your Father, Dreaming

"Your father is on the train of ghosts," we said, imagining our various fathers.
And when the train pulls up to the station, and you board,
the idea is that he'll be there, that he'll put down the newspaper he'd been reading,
and smile, waving you to a seat. He'll say something about seeing you
    on the platform
from the window as the train approached,
that on the way into the city, he saw people on their rooftops,
hanging Christmas lights. He'll say he feels these days like he's an Apollo astronaut,
one of the ones who circled the moon but never landed.
                                       Last night
I dreamt I entered a bridge on-ramp too fast, too close to the railing,
as I was trying to see if this is the Big Dipper I'm seeing or the Little Dipper.
It looked off, half-erased. And then the railing was coming at me.
My cousin Lyle, a few months before he died, angry at the party
in the adjacent apartment, shot up their door with his pellet gun.
They never knew, as it was a pellet gun, leaving no more than a few scratch marks,
something a cat or dog might leave. We lost contact after that,
and then next thing I know, he's on the train, twenty-eight.
"What do you want to be, for real?" your father asks, still holding the newspaper.
It's an old paper, lamenting the panic and violence of 1968,
the "year of the barricades." "History,"
he says, "is littered with examples of things that seemed like good ideas
at the time, but turned out to be disastrous."
                                  "I never knew you,"
you can say in response, but it feels unfair, the outskirts of the city
going by, the weather turning lovely
out the windows.
                I want to think I'll be a good father,
that I'll wait on the train for my children, with a newspaper,
that I'll put it down as they approach, and welcome them.
It just gets like that, the dreaming. "We are now approaching lunar sunrise,"

Bill Anders is saying over the intercom, "and for all the people back on Earth, the crew of Apollo 8 has a message that we would like to send to you."
For him, it's December 24, 1968,
the most-watched television broadcast of the era,
and he's about to read from the book of Genesis, 100 miles above the moon.

Running

I want to talk in ideas, but all I have are words. I want to fold
into ideas, float, like the idea of The Adopted Child,
or the idea that there's only one subject
going by different names. It's the feeling I have when running,
the urge to not stop, with my various strategies of crossing roads,
weaving, adjusting distance and speed, which upsets drivers. Dale,
an off-duty highway patrolman/ high school soccer coach,
rolled his window down and made a "cut the shit" gesture
the other day, that I decided to take as a wave, before waving back,
because I'll never be a local, no matter how long I'm here,
and feigning misunderstanding is my tent pole. People
can sense that, like a pretend accent, which summarizes my interactions
with Dale. They love saying, when I run past, that whoever
is chasing me has stopped. I wave, out of breath, and no,
it's the future chasing me. It's right here. Look. As pursuit
is chase as well as occupation, and it follows
in the same category as persecution and prosecution,
all senses of which one finds in fairytales, how children
are abandoned, and they wander, trying to act good, to get
somewhere safe, only to find they've ended up in an oven
tended by an evil stepmother. I'm sorry, stepmothers of the world,
that this is what it's come to. Like how a lion, when it takes over
as head lion, will kill the young of its predecessor. No adoptees
allowed. You protect your line. You're the royal houses of Europe now.
And here, near the end of the idea, I'm running down Icon
Road. Fall. 48 degrees. Drizzle. Sometimes the child's cursed, marked,
ill-omened, parented by supernatural beings. It's a devil,
changeling swapped by fairies, prophesied to destroy parents,
community, civilization. The stories most likely come

from historical accounts of parents defending infanticide—a difficult
pregnancy, a birth on a day with bad connotations or into a family
with already too many children—because there are so many things
for a person to keep track of, so one thinks of it as fate,
tidal forces moving across the land, thinks they're part
of an epic, our sin is our salvation. We've seen what those people can do,
so I keep running, little changeling, little gingerbread man.

How's It Going

"How's it going?" I ask, opening up the genealogy website. Like we're
at a show. Like "Good evening, Springfield! It's great to be back!"
I'm tired of myself and this pile of names and dates.
But I want to know, in the "kind of" way we'd like to know
when we say, "How's it going?" as everything we are
is a billboard we step out of or into. I probably just need to relax,
open a clear space. And space says, "How's it going?"
"Things are best," some aunt or uncle or cousin says, "when one
doesn't think so much about the past." And that means they know
something they don't want to tell you. Or they suspect
something they don't want to tell you. Or maybe they just
don't care so much. The diving board hesitates. The flies
following you home hesitate. And to understand that, we have to say
"how's it going" when passing each other in hallways. It's a way

of combing your hair. It's a formal address to the architecture.
How's it going? In asking, our competition is obituaries.
Our competition is every year a new color. 2022
is Very Peri. Fine, and you? 2023 was unveiled today
by Pantone. It's Viva Magenta. That's how it's going.
What do the days of the week feel like to birds?
Why doesn't the music we grew up listening to relate to this afternoon?
The old music asks, "How's it going?" That's how
it goes. It's a way of looking down a circular flight of stairs.
Like asking what the best way to be anxious is.
Like Springfield, Missouri-Ohio-Massachusetts-Illinois.
And what then is a wasted life and what is a meaningful one?
Like going to the haunted ghost town in a closed
amusement park. Like a model train town with painted sky.

Dress Rehearsals

I keep dreaming I've killed someone and I can't remember
where I put the body. And we're having guests over
this weekend. What to do?
We'd love to sell the house. Who wouldn't love
to get rid of this house? It's so hard to get rid of things.
Like really get rid of them, all these anthologies
guest edited by Halloween. If you stand just right,
you can see both shorelines. The garden.
Have I checked the garden? Math problem.
If my father died last spring, the house would be worth $200,000.
Now it's worth 125. Do you want to sell?
You could fit a swimming pool here. But maybe not so much digging.
Maybe it's worth 150. Just wait a bit,
the paint changes color as it dries.
Everyone who ever lived is jumping into the Grand Canyon,
which is still not filled. There's a frantic applesauce about it, though.
Like maybe why is everyone jumping into it.
I'm writing my father's obituary. It's a new genre for me.
As identity is a genre. I wonder if they have a *Best American
Obituaries* yearly anthology. Maybe this will get into it. It goes
like this: that's all there is. You build some roads. They're
all right. Most people say it as one word, *alright*.
I don't know what I'm supposed to do.
The neighbor's dogs are sniffing around the garage.
Actually, those are my dogs. Maybe I should call someone and say
it feels like prayer but not like praying.
He wants a pine box. Of course he wants a pine box. Probably
one made by Boy Scouts, singing, "My Country 'Tis of Thee."

The way the hospital scene is always the hospital scene.

This room looks contagious.

No one saw me just do this amazing parking job.

As long as I don't get out of the car, everything's fine.

We'll All Be Dead by Morning

Only one cell is meant to outlast us. So we sing songs about the sea.
We imagine heaven. And by the same gesture, none of these things
around the room are meant to outlast us, though at some point,
all of them do, and we end up with a dead relative's car
or refrigerator. It's the body, suddenly, how we're nourished
and how we get from point A to point B, and there it is,
that one cell, if you've had children. It's sitting in your car
singing along with Fleetwood Mac's "Second Hand News"
or it's reaching up behind the orange juice for the picante sauce.

Maybe you've thought this before, and you're losing patience
with how I'm just getting to it. If so, I'm sorry. Generations
do this, and I was so young a few moments ago.
                                                    We climb back
from the long string of DNA, and say something like "the band
has retaken the stage," and it could be we're at a concert
or we're in a western movie, high wind, dust, and I vote
for a concert right now, where two of the four players seem
to nearly fall asleep in the middle break, it's so beautiful.

Maybe it's Neil Young and Crazy Horse, 1970, playing "Cowgirl
in the Sand" so that, in a way, it's still a western movie,
and the stage is on fire and many people are shooting
and getting shot behind rocks. Your great-great grandfather
is there and he's just been hit. I'm sorry to have to bring you
this news, that he makes it no further,
                                                    except for this one cell,
littered with distant planets and the solitary measure of day

becoming night when all manner of things move around
and become catering kitchens and ponies, language theory
and occupied countries for class on Monday, questions four
through eight in your notebooks, emptying and reloading
the dishwasher, putting some pans in the sink to soak.

The Wizard of Oz Museum

There's a theory of life in what you're doing at this moment,
a conception of things. And we get used to it, how I'd been dwelling all my life
in wanting to know my birth mother's name.
It became my definition of self, a house
of vacant rooms. And then one Thursday, it's answered,
simple as a wind-up doll, as saying hi on an elevator
or dropping a pen, as if all things culminate.
Like I had this truck I loved. Toyota T100 long bed.
I could fit a full sheet of drywall in the back, flat. I did that only once,
but there's a definition in knowing I could. And then this old guy
in a Toyota Camry runs a stop sign. I get a new truck, new
definition of self, and Boyd's looking forward to being sixteen
and getting it. But it's old already. It'll be five more years
until he's sixteen. Intersections are everywhere.
Our kitchen sink is growing difficult. Winter whistles
through the rooms. The floor lilts. What we plan falls apart
some Saturday when the blue spruce falls through the back porch.

We went to the Gallaher family reunion in Monterey, and found
it was the same weekend as *The Wizard of Oz* convention,
while milling about the gazebo with the Tin Man and Scarecrow.
"Family is the family you make," reads the message
they slip under your hotel room door. When you're adopted,
it's always happening. Dorothy's talking too loud,
or maybe it's that everyone thinks they're Dorothy,
a chorus line of Dorothys getting the best song. "We're on a journey,"
the yellow brick road says. The Wizard replies, "A heart is not judged
by how much you love; but by how much you are loved."
And what criteria are they using? Where's the checklist?

Today Is One of the Days of the Week

I know a few things. One, bananas are radioactive. Blame
potassium. Blame the little-talked about facts
about how bad everything is for you. Another, I'm in the fifth decade
of my angsty teen phase. One of the joys of travel
is you can pretend you're someone else, and you're anywhere.
When no one can see me, I'm Steve McQueen.
How about a feigned accent at gas stations? Yes, please.
Funny thing: my father dies, and when I get to the community guard gate,
my name isn't on the "OK People" list. I promise, Gate Guard,
it's OK I go to his empty house and go through his things for the next three days.
At some point, no one is interested in your prized possessions.
Therefore, I'm trying not to be a broom. I want to be a safe.
But you don't always get what you want. Or
what you need, either. The Rolling Stones were wrong on that,
we all know it, and who's talking about it? The trees?
At the funeral, next to the church, some guys were burning stuff
in the backyard of a house, in a dumpster, being metaphorical,
the smoke going gray then white, and I imagined
they'd just elected a new pope. "In the presence of your creator,"
the priest said. This week I was in a traffic jam
heading into a dazzling sunset. Even with my eyes closed,
it's everywhere. During the week of the funeral
I listened to 408 songs from this year, including remasters
of Pavement and The Beatles. The Beatles' album, *Revolver*,
sounds as if it was just recorded. "As if"
is a handy phrase. Hear it the way I hear it: Rita
makes a speech at the burial about barren women,
about how she's a barren woman, as my mother was,
and "barren women have to adopt." And the children
they adopt, she says, they love "as if

they were their very own." The temperature is dropping all day.
It was fall. It will be winter by midnight. As if
over a cocoon. As if
we will grow wings and circle the flowers of summer.

The Book of Names

And suddenly everyone's friendly. We're working in the front yard,
Boyd and I, and our neighbor who's never spoken to us, calls out
"Good job!" And now we're talking. She's 77. "Early spring,"
she says, and then "my grandkids can't come up to visit, because."
We nod. We're nodders. We wave. We're wavers. For years,
our dog would never stop barking until he passed out. And now, people pass,
saying things like "your dog has a lot of energy!"
We even had him trained once. The trainer didn't admit defeat,
but came close. It's turned into another scrap in our box of receipts,
which I now want to find. I want his telephone number.
I want to tell him it's OK. We all fail. We failed
in continuing the training. Success goes to the one who will do
what no one else will, and we didn't. Everything is close,
the soft hug of it, whispering our flux of days, my year-end evaluation,
the last handful of jelly beans, who do I remember from high school:
test your skills. I've started saying, "Hi, neighbor" to trees and mailboxes.
Someone finds a planet that rotates its star every nine hours.
I imagine doing the math of how old I'd be there. Hey, neighbor,
I think, waving at a point in the sky I imagine that planet to be.
Your year is so long now. All our years are long. All our years
are the same year, mirrored up and down the block. Even the birds
are closer. They've taken to landing on the porch rail
I painted white two summers ago that needs to be repainted already.
"To know is to seek to know," I whisper to them
from the kitchen window, imagining I'm writing Ecclesiastes.
My neighbor's passing again. It's a good walking street. We say, "Hi again!"
and laugh. I'm busy naming the trees Luke, Alice, Nicole.
"What will the future think?" we ask, when all we can see
is the present. We take pictures, hoping we'll look OK.

ACKNOWLEDGMENTS

Grateful acknowledgment to the editors of the following journals in which these poems appeared, sometimes in earlier versions:

32 Poems

Academy of American Poets

AGNI

American Poetry Review

Bear Review

BOAAT

Colorado Review

Copper Nickel

Court Green

Crazyhorse

The Florida Review

The Glacier

Hotel Amerika

I-70 Review

Lake Effect

LIPS

The Missouri Review

New Ohio Review

Ninth Letter

Pleiades

Ploughshares

Plume

Puerto Del Sol

Redactions

Radar Poetry

River Styx

Southern Indiana Review

Sugar House Review

Typo

Washington Square Review

Waxwing

Many people helped in the writing of this book. Robin, Boyd, Natalie, for their support; Marie Carvalho in the research and finding; Luke Rolfes, Daniel Biegelson, G.C. Waldrep, Kate Nuernberger, Richard Sonnenmoser, David Dodd Lee, Kevin Craft, Chris Banks, in the thinking and writing; Pat Gorman, Dan Graff, Gary Ferrington, Ken Gorman, Richard Gallaher for talking; and to Ryan Travis, thank you. Special thank you to Martha Rhodes for seeing a book in this, Ryan Murphy for designing it, and Hannah Matheson and Shoshauna Shy for organizing and editing it into existence. And to Shane McCrae and Erin Belieu in the final stages.

ABOUT THE AUTHOR

John Gallaher teaches at Northwest Missouri State University and co-edits the *Laurel Review*. A previous winner of the Levis Award and The Boston Review Prize, his poems have appeared in *The Best American Poetry, Poetry, The American Poetry Review*, and others. The author of five previous collections of poetry, Gallaher has also co-written books with G.C. Waldrep and Kristina Marie Darling, and co-edited collections with Mary Biddinger and Laura Boss.

PUBLICATION OF THIS BOOK WAS MADE POSSIBLE
BY GRANTS AND DONATIONS. WE ARE ALSO GRATEFUL
TO THOSE INDIVIDUALS WHO PARTICIPATED IN
OUR BUILD A BOOK PROGRAM. THEY ARE:

Anonymous (14), Robert Abrams, Michael Ansara, Kathy Aponick, Jean Ball, Sally Ball, Clayre Benzadon, Adrian Blevins, Laurel Blossom, Adam Bohannon, Betsy Bonner, Patricia Bottomley, Lee Briccetti, Joel Brouwer, Susan Buttenwieser, Anthony Cappo, Paul and Brandy Carlson, Dan Clarke, Mark Conway, Elinor Cramer, Kwame Dawes, Michael Anna de Armas, John Del Peschio, Brian Komei Dempster, Rosalynde Vas Dias, Patrick Donnelly, Lynn Emanuel, Blas Falconer, Jennifer Franklin, John Gallaher, Reginald Gibbons, Rebecca Kaiser Gibson, Dorothy Tapper Goldman, Julia Guez, Naomi Guttman and Jonathan Mead, Forrest Hamer, Luke Hankins, Yona Harvey, KT Herr, Karen Hildebrand, Carlie Hoffman, Glenna Horton, Thomas and Autumn Howard, Catherine Hoyser, Elizabeth Jackson, Linda Susan Jackson, Jessica Jacobs and Nickole Brown, Lee Jenkins, Elizabeth Kanell, Nancy Kassell, Maeve Kinkead, Victoria Korth, Brett Lauer and Gretchen Scott, Howard Levy, Owen Lewis and Susan Ennis, Margaree Little, Sara London and Dean Albarelli, Tariq Luthun, Myra Malkin, Louise Mathias, Victoria McCoy, Lupe Mendez, Michael and Nancy Murphy, Kimberly Nunes, Susan Okie and Walter Weiss, Cathy McArthur Palermo, Veronica Patterson, Jill Pearlman, Marcia and Chris Pelletiere, Sam Perkins, Susan Peters and Morgan Driscoll, Maya Pindyck, Megan Pinto, Kevin Prufer, Martha Rhodes and Jean Brunel, Paula Rhodes, Louise Riemer, Peter and Jill Schireson, Rob Schlegel, Yoana Setzer, Soraya Shalforoosh, Mary Slechta, Diane Souvaine, Barbara Spark, Catherine Stearns, Jacob Strautmann, Yerra Sugarman, Arthur Sze and Carol Moldaw, Marjorie and Lew Tesser, Dorothy Thomas, Rushi Vyas, Martha Webster and Robert Fuentes, Rachel Weintraub and Allston James, Abby Wender and Rohan Weerasinghe, and Monica Youn.